ESSENTIAL LATIN VOCABULARY

THE 1,425 MOST COMMON WORDS
OCCURRING IN THE ACTUAL WRITINGS
OF OVER 200 LATIN AUTHORS

By
Mark A. E. Williams

Based upon the works of
P. Diederich, Gonzalez Lodge, et al.

SOPHRON

2012

in cooperation with

E.G.Inkwell

California, United States of America

ISBN-13: 978-0615702506

ISBN-10: 0615702503

Design by **Sophron**

in cooperation with

E.G.Inkwell

California, United States of America

Contents

Abbreviations

Abl	ablative
ac	active
Acc	accusative
adj	adjective
adv	adverb
cnj	conjunction
Dcl	declension
Dt, Dat	dative
F, Fm, Fem	feminine
Fut	future
FutPerf	future perfect
Gn, Gen	genitive
Imprf	Imperfect
ind	indeclinable
int	interjection
irr	irregular
M, Masc	masculine
n	noun
Nm, Nom	nomnitive
Nt, Neut	neuter
P, Pl	Plural
PlPerf, PluPerf	pluperfect
Pr	present
Prf	perfect
pro	pronoun
prp	preposition
Ps	passive
S, Sing	singular
Sbj, Subj	subjunctive
sbst, subst	substantive
smtms	sometimes
v	verb
%m	permilliage (per 1,000)

PREFACE

This study book has come to completion due in no small part to the support and encouragement of Mr. Giles Laurén at Sophron. He has been an extremely valuable guide and a source of assistance along the way, pointing out any number of places where I might have gone astray, and greatly improving the final text.

I owe a significant further debt to Dr. Mark Riley, Professor Emeritus at California State University, Sacramento. Proofreading a text of this sort is tedious in the extreme, but he graciously undertook that work for a generous portion of the book. The errors and oversights he found would have been misleading to students and embarrassing to me. His remarks were detailed, knowledgable, and extraordinarily helpful.

Finally, Mr. Nathan Thompson offered helpful critiques on early drafts of the text. Undaunted by this experience, he later agreed to read over a proof of this book and to work with it in order to test its viability in real studies. He too has found errors and offered comments that improved both content and presentation of the material here. To him, as well, I owe my sincere thanks.

The responsibility for any remaining mistakes or misjudgments is, of course, my own. With that in mind, any comments, criticism, or further corrections will be gratefully received at EssentialLatin@gmail.com.

M.A.E.W.

For **Jutta**, uxorcula

Vitium vitae,
in aula Dei
scurraque,
super faciem terrae
erroque sum.

Et ego non magis possum
te bene amare
quam umbrae cantare
possunt.

Sed,
non multum edo,
rarenter interpello,
et numquam
lodices clepo.

Me tenebis?

September, 2012

HOW TO USE THIS BOOK

This book is designed to help beginning and intermediate students master the vocabulary necessary to read real Latin with fluency and comprehension. It also serves as a resource for instructors and tutors. The text presents 1,425 words that allow a student to comprehend about 95% of all the vocabulary they will ever see in an actual Latin text. Most of the remaining 5% can be worked out through context, or deduced by the fact they are compounds of the given words. These 1,425 words encompass the standard Latin vocabulary of the General Certificate for Secondary Education, as well, even when the GCSE terms do not occur frequently enough to warrant inclusion on statistical grounds alone.

The terms found in the present book have been culled from statistical analyses involving hundreds of thousands of words taken from a broad range of more than two hundred authors in order to identify the most frequently occurring core vocabulary. The backbone of this research lies within the unpublished dissertation of Paul Diederich, but I have completely reordered his terms into the traditional grammatical settings that students will more easily recognise.[1] I have also dropped some terms he found significant and added others which proved more reliably frequent in later, larger studies[2] of vocabulary frequency.

Definitions provided here are also adaptations of those found in Diederich. In fact, a great many definitions — perhaps most of them — have been taken from Gonzales Lodge's work,[3] though the standard lexicons have been used as well. Finally, I have taken

---

[1]Paul Diederich's 1939 dissertation at the University of Chicago largely sought to redefine the grammatical structures under which Latin was taught in schools. This makes part of his work less accessible to contemporary students.

[2]A number of these have been done. See, e.g., the *Dictionnaire Fréquentiel et Index Inverse de la Langue Latine*, Laboratoire d'Analyse statistique des Langues anciennes, Université de Liège, 1981.

[3] See Gonzales Lodge's *Vocabulary of High School Latin*, New York: Teachers College Columbia Universtiy, 1922.

some smaller liberties in arranging the Topical Groups compiled by Diederich.

Leaning on vocabulary frequency as a guide to increasing a student's reading accuracy and fluency should not be underestimated. For example, were students to start out by learning the 25 most common words on this list, an astonishing 29% of all the vocabulary ever needed would be at their command. If a student masters the 300 most frequent words in this list, about 58% of all the vocabulary necessary for fluent reading will be theirs.

The goal of the book is to provide the student with the most efficient way to learn vocabulary. This is done by grouping the same terms into different sets. There is one set in each chapter. The first two chapters, in particular, are designed for drill, review, and study. The first chapter draws together all words that share the same grammatical classification. For example, all third declension neuter nouns are brought together in one place, with their definitions. All verbs of the second conjugation are defined in a separate list. By listing the vocabulary in grammatical groups, all the words that share a set of endings are thus assembled for the student; endings and vocabulary can reinforce each other.

This grammatical grouping has the added bonus of creating realistic subsets of terms that can be mastered over a few days. There are, for example, only 73 second conjugation verbs. There are only 56 second declension masculine nouns. By focusing on one such group, all of which share the same inflections, the endings can be reinforced while an entire vocabulary group is mastered in relatively short order. By learning eight words a day, for example, the whole scope of second declension masculine nouns will be mastered, in all their forms, within a week.

At the head of each list within the grammatical set, the lexical forms are given, and, where practical, the most basic endings are listed for quick review (though an entire chapter is devoted to paradigms later in the book). Furthermore, each list of terms will be further broken down into groups of five words for ease in drawing up vocabulary lists for memorization.

Within the grammatical lists, each part of speech is preceded by an account of how the terms within are distributed. A student thus quickly learns that while there are 413 verbs that need to be mastered, well over one-third of these (156) are found in the third conjugation, while only about one per-cent (21) will be found in the fourth conjugation. Third declension nouns account for 190 of the 450 nouns that should be mastered. With such information, beginning students can focus their attention on those endings that will cover most of the vocabulary they will need to know.

But this grammatical grouping is only the first chapter. In the second chapter, large parts of the vocabulary, with their attendant definitions, are regrouped by topics. A student who wishes, therefore, to focus on nature, or human emotions, or military issues, will find such vocabulary conveniently grouped together should they wish to study their words topically.

Chapter three lists the vocabulary terms from the most frequently occurring words to the least frequent. Students or instructors who wish to lean more heavily on the most (or least!) frequently occurring terms within their drills and studies can thus consult this frequency list, recalling that the first 25 words account for a bit less than one-third of all terms needed, and the first 300 words account for over half of the vocabulary necessary for reading actual Latin authors.

After the frequency list, the fourth chapter presents an alphabetical index of the terms. Here, one can look up any term and discover which grammatical list it will be found on, as well as its topical list, where appropriate. In addition, the frequency is given here again, so one might look up the term in the frequency list and discover other words used at about the same rate.

Two final chapters close the text. The first is a list of endings and paradigms for nouns, adjectives and verbs. Complete paradigms and endings are given for review.

Finally, the book closes with an additional one hundred words that are uniquely common in the Latin of the Middle Ages. These one hundred words, if added to the mix, would give the student a Mediaeval vocabulary that would match the efficiency of the

Classical vocabulary that is the main focus of the book. Furthermore, many of these Mediaeval terms are quite easily recognised and mastered: clericus, monasterium, angelus, to take just a few examples. For the effort of learning an additional one-hundred words, another 1,000 years of Latin texts open up before the student. As Paul Diederich observes in his dissertation, the Latin of the Middle Ages is authentic Latin, penned by those who daily spoke, read, and thought in the language. It is a literature that offers the student the "glamour of the unexplored" and frequently contains relatively simple texts that can be ideal for early students making their first transitions from school book exercises to authentic Latin. For all these reasons the inclusion of the Mediaeval List of common Latin terms seemed advisable.

As a whole, then, this book offers the vocabulary that forms the core of one thousand seven hundred years of Latin literature.

If the goal is to learn to read Latin with joy and ease, then the 1,425 vocabulary terms in this book are one of the major keys to success. By learning these terms, a student's vocabulary should be ready to tackle the Latin of any era from the Classical period to the Renaissance.

Chapter 1

Grammatical Lists

For nouns, verbs and adjectives, the basic inflections are presented in a table at the head of each list. The endings listed in the lexicon are highlighted for ease of reference.

Nouns

Nouns occur in five declensions. Of the 1,325 most common words in Classical Latin, 450 (just under 34%) are nouns. The student will find them distributed as follows:

Declension	Masc	Fem	Neut	Total
First	4	83	0	87
Second	56	1	75	132
Third*	73	75	42	190
Fourth	25	3	1	29
Fifth	1	8	0	9
Indecl.	0	3	0	3
Totals	159	173	118	450

*Fourteen third declension nouns may be either masculine or feminine depending on context. They are here tallied with the masculine nouns; in the lists below, they are shown separately.

FIRST DECLENSION

	NOM	ACC	GEN	DAT	ABL
Sing	-a	-am	-ae	-ae	-ā
Plur	-ae	-ās	-ārum	-īs	-īs

Masculine (-a, -ae)   [4 nouns]

agricola, -ae	farmer, field worker
nauta, -ae	sailor
poēta, -ae	poet
scurra, -ae	fool, jester, commedian

Feminine (-a -ae)   [83 nouns]

amīcitia, -ae	friendship
ancilla, -ae	slave-girl, slave-woman
anima, -ae	breeze; air; breath, spirit; life, soul (esp. in plural)
aqua, -ae	water
āra, -ae	altar
aura, -ae	breeze, breath of air; gleam; vapor; (Pl) airs, heaven
causa, -ae	cause, motive; origin; occasion, subject; lawsuit, trial
cēna, -ae	dinner, meal
clēmentia, -ae	gentleness, mildness
coma, -ae	hair, tresses
cōpia, -ae	plenty, supply, abundance; (Pl) forces, esp. troops; supplies
corōna, -ae	garland, chaplet, wreath
culpa, -ae	guilt, fault, blame
cūra, -ae	care, worry, concern
dea, -ae	goddess; Dt & Ab Pl *smtms* deābus

dīvitiae, -ārum	riches (Pl only)
domina, -ae	householder, mistress, lady
epistula, -ae	letter
extera, -ae	female foreigner
fābula, -ae	a fictitious narrative, tale, story; dramatic poem, play; fable
fāma, -ae	rumor, reputation; fame, glory
fēmina, -ae	woman
fera, -ae	wild animal
figūra, -ae	form, shape
fīlia, -ae	daughter; Dt & Ab Pl *smtms* filiābus
flamma, -ae	flame, fire
fōrma, -ae	form, figure; structure, appearance; beauty
fortūna, -ae	fortune
fuga, -ae	flight, a running away, a route
gena, -ae	cheek, eye
glōria, -ae	glory, fame
grātia, -ae	favour; influence; gratitude; the Graces
herba, -ae	herb; grass, turf, plan; meadow
hōra, -ae	hour
iniūria, -ae	injustice, wrong, affront
īnsidia, -ae	a plot; treachery; trap; (Pl) ambush, ambuscade
insula, -ae	island; block of flats
invidia, -ae	envy, jealousy, hatred
īra, -ae	anger, wrath
iuventa, -ae	period of youth, youth
lacrima, -ae	tear
lingua, -ae	tongue; language
littera, -ae	letter (of the alphabet); (Pl) literature, epistle, letters
lūna, -ae	moon

lyra, -ae	a lute, lyre; lyric poetry, song; the constellation Lyra
māteria, -ae	timber, lumber
memoria, -ae	memory, recollection; history; that within memory; tradition
mēnsa, -ae	table
mora, -ae	delay, hindrance; pause
mūsa, -ae	muse 50
nātūra, -ae	nature
nympha, -ae	nymph
opera, -ae	work, care; aid; service, effort
ōra, -ae	coast
pātria, -ae	fatherland, country
pecūnia, -ae	money
philosophia, -ae	philosophy, love of wisdom
poena, -ae	penalty, punishment
potentia, -ae	force, power
porta, -ae	gate
praeda, -ae	booty, prey
prōvincia, -ae	province; office
puella, -ae	girl; maiden
pugna, -ae	battle, fight
rēgīna, -ae	queen
rīpa, -ae	bank (of a river)
rosa, -ae	rose
rota, -ae	wheel
ruīna, -ae	downfall, collapse
sapientia, -ae	wisdom; judgment, understanding; reason
sententia, -ae	feeling, thinking, opinion, judgment, &c.
silva, -ae	forest, grove
stēlla, -ae	star

taberna, -ae	shop, inn, tavern
tenebrae, -ārum	darkness (Pl only)
terra, -ae	land (as opp. to water, air)
turba, -ae	confusion, tumult; crowd, throng
umbra, -ae	shade, shadow
unda, -ae	wave, billow; sea
via, -ae	way, route, street
victōria, -ae	victory
vīlla, -ae	country-seat
vīta, -ae	life

SECOND DECLENSION

Masculine and feminine endings are identical.

	NOM	ACC	GEN	DAT	ABL
Sing	**-us***	-um	**-ī**	-ō	-ō
Plur	-ī	-ōs	-ōrum	-īs	-īs

*Stems that end in -r or in -er will drop the -us in the Nm S.

Masculine (-us, -ī)   *[56 nouns]*

ager, agrī	cultivated land, field, country
amīcus, -ī	friend
animus, -ī	feeling, spirit, soul
annus, -ī	year
barbarus, -ī	foreigner, stranger (of all but Greeks and Romans)
campus, -ī	plain, field
capillus, -ī	head of hair, hair
captīvus, -ī	captive, prisoner of war

chorus, -ī	dance, choral dance; band, troop
cibus, -ī	food
deus, -ī	god
digitus, -ī	finger
dominus, -ī	householder, master, lord
equus, -ī	horse
fīlius, -ī	son
gladius, -ī	sword (the prose word)
hortus, -ī	garden
inimīcus, ī	personal enemy
legatus, -ī	envoy, ambassador; commander of a legion; officer
libellus, -ī	booklet
liber -brī	book, volume; inner bark of the tree
līberī, -ōrum	children (pl only)
lībertus, -ī	freedman, ex-slave
locus, -ī	place, location (pl is Nt: -a -ōrum); pl loci -ōrum: passages in a book
lūcus, -ī	grove; sacred grove
magister, -trī	master, schoolmaster; foreman, chief; steersman
marītus, -ī	husband, married man; lover, suitor
minister, -trī	attendant, servant; tool, agent
modus, -ī	measure, manner, kind
morbus, -ī	sickness, disease
mundus, -ī	universe, the world; the earth; the inhabitants of the earth, mankind
mūrus, -ī	wall
nātus, -ī	son; (of animals) a young one; (Pl) offspring; *smtms*: nāta, -ae, f., for daughter
numerus, -ī	number, amount; rhythm
nūntius, -ī	messenger; message, news
oculus, -ī	eye
polus, -ī	pole (extremity of an axis); sky, heavens

pontus, -ī	the open sea, deep
populus, -ī	people; nation
puer, puerī	boy; slave; (Pl) children
rāmus, -ī	branch, bough (of a tree)
rogus, -ī	funeral pyre
servus, -ī	slave
socius, -ī	ally, confederate
somnus, -ī	sleep
sonus, -ī	sound, noise
taurus, -ī	bull
thalamus, -ī	bed-chamber, couch, (esp.) bridal bed
titulus, -ī	inscription, label, title; notice, bill, placard; honourable appellation, title; pretext
torus, -ī	bed, couch; royal seat or throne 50
tribunus, -ī	tribune
triumphus, -ī	triumph
tumulus, -ī	hillock, mound; swelling
ventus, -ī	wind
vīcīnus, -ī	neighbour
vir, virī	man; husband; hero

II. Feminine (-us, -ī) [1 noun]

humus, -ī	ground

7

II. Neuter (-um, -ī)   [75 nouns]

	NOM	ACC	GEN	DAT	ABL
Sing	-um	-um	-ī	-ō	-ō
Plur	-a	-a	-ōrum	-īs	-īs

aevum, -ī	lifetime, age, old age; eternity
antrum, -ī	cave, cavern, grot
arma, -orum	(Pl only) arms, armor; implements of war; gear, tackle
arvum, -ī	field; plowed land
astrum, -ī	heavenly body, star, planet; constellation; sky
aurum, -ī	gold; money
auxilium, -ī	support, assistance; (Pl) auxiliary forces, reinforcements
bellum, -ī	war
beneficium, -ī	kindness, favor, privilege
bonum, -ī	good, good thing; profit, advantage; material goods, supplies
caelum, -ī	sky; heaven
castra, -ōrum	camp, military encampment (Pl only)
ceteri, ceterorum	the others, the rest; all the rest; (Pl) from ceterus, used as a subst.
collum, -ī	neck
cōnsilium, -ī	plan, idea, advice; council, deliberative body; prudence, discretion
dōnum, -ī	gift, present
exemplum, -ī	pattern; copy; analogy; archetype; reproduction, transcrption
exsilium, -ī	exile, banishment; those exiled (Pl)
factum, -ī	fact, deed, act; accomplishment, achievement
fātum, -ī	fate (lit. that which is spoken)
ferrum, -ī	iron; iron tool; weapon, sword

forum, -ī	market-place; Roman forum; place of public meeting
fretum, -ī	strait (of water)
gaudium, -ī	delight, joy, pleasure
imperium, -ī	empire, power, command
incendium, -ī	conflagration; glow, heat
ingenium, -ī	character; temperament; ability
initium, -ī	beginning, commencement; entrance
iudicium, -ī	judgment, decision; opinion; trial
iugum, -ī	yoke; ridge, chain of hills; summit
lētum, -ī	ruin; (poetry) death
malum, -ī	evil, mischief; disaster; harm; also: apple
membrum, -ī	member, limb, organ; male genitals; room; section
monumentum, -ī	reminder; memorial, monument
negotium, -ī	pain, trouble, distress; work, business, activity, job
odium, -ī	hatred; unpopularity; boredom, impatience
officium, -ī	service, duty; kindness
oppidum, -ī	town
ōsculum, -ī	kiss
ōtium, -ī	leisure
pelagus, -ī	sea (esp. the open sea)
perīculum, -ī	danger, peril
pōculum, -ī	drinking cup
praeceptum, -ī	lesson, teaching, precept; command, order
praemium, -ī	bounty, reward
praesidium, -ī	protection; help; guard; garrison
pretium, -ī	price
prīncipium, -ī	beginning
proelium, -ī	fight, battle
rēgnum, -ī	royal power; control; kingdom 50

9

sacrum, -ī	sacrifice; sacred vessel; (Pl) religious rites
saeculum, -ī	a generation; age, esp. century; time in general
saxum, -ī	stone; stone face, cliff
sepulcrum, -ī	place of burial, tomb, grave
sertum, -ī	wreath of flowers, garland
sīgnum, -ī	sign, signal; mark, a seal; military standard
somnium, -ī	dream
spatium, -ī	space (of time, usually; *smtms:* of place)
studium, -ī	eagerness, devotion; (Pl) pursuits
supplicium, -ī	punishment, suffering; supplication; torture
tēctum, -ī	a covered place; roof; building, house
tēlum, -ī	weapon; bolt, javelin
templum, -ī	temple, holy place; place marked off for augury
tergum, -ī	back, rear
vadum, -ī	a ford; shallows, a shoal
vēlum, -ī	a cloth, covering; esp. sail
venēnum, -ī	poison; drug
verbum, -ī	word
verum, -ī	truth, reality, fact; verum as adv: yes, in truth, indeed
vestīgium, -ī	footstep, footprint, track, trace
vinculum, -ī	bond, fetter, tie
vīnum, -ī	wine; vine
vitium, -ī	flaw, defect, foible; crime
vōtum, -ī	vow, sacred promise; prayer; sacred offering; vote
vulgus, -ī	the common people

THIRD DECLENSION

Masculine (--, -is) [*59 nouns*]

	NOM	ACC	GEN	DAT	ABL
Sing	--	-em	**-is**	-ī	-e
Plur	-ēs	-ēs	-(i)um*	-ibus	-ibus

*The *-i-* of the Gen Pl ending is unpredictable and may or may not appear in any given word. There is no simple rule that will guarantee success in this matter.

aethēr, -eris	pure upper air, ether, heaven, sky
amnis, -is	river, torrent
amor, -ōris	love
cinis, -eris	ashes, embers
clāmor, -ōris	outcry, shout
collis, -is	hill
color, -ōris	color
cōnsul, -is	consul
crīnis, -is	hair; locke of hair; plume of a helmet; tail of a comet
dīves, -itis	the rich; those who are well off; (Gn Pl -um)
dolor, -ōris	pain, grief; sorrow; resentment
dux, ducis	leader, guide, general
eques, -itis	horseman, rider; (Pl) cavalry; equestrian order
error, -ōris	wandering; error, mistake, deception
fīnis, -is	end point, termination; boundary
flōs, -ōris	flower, blossom; bloom; prime of youth
fōns, fontis	spring, fountain
frāter, -tris	brother
furor, -ōris	rage; fury

11

grex, gregis	herd
gurges, -itis	gulf, whirlpool; sea
homō, -inis	person, man
honor, -ōris	honor, praise, glory
hospes, -itis	host; guest, visitor, stranger; soldier in billets
hymen, -is	wedding chant; wedding; as a proper name: god of marriage
ignis, -is	fire
imber, -bris	rain-storm, shower
imperātor, -ōris	commander, general
iūdex, -icis	judge, juror, arbiter
labor, -ōris	toil, exertion
lapis, -idis	stone
lar, laris	Lares (Gn Pl -um or -ium); god(s) of the home, hearth, household
leō, -ōnis	lion
mēnsis, -is	month
mercātor, -oris	merchant
mīles, -itis	soldier
mōns, montis	mountain
mōs, mōris	manner, way, custom, habit
nēmō, -inis	no one, nobody
nepōs, -ōtis	grandson; descendant; spendthrift, prodigal, playboy
ōrātor, -ōris	pleader, orator, spokesman
orbis, -is	circle; territory; sphere
ōrdō, -inis	succession, order, class, rank, row, &c.
pater, -tris	father
pauper, -eris	a poor person
pēs, pedis	foot
prīnceps, -ipis	the first person on a list; the one who originates, first delivers, or declares, an opinion; the first, the most eminent, most distinguished
pudor, -ōris	shame, modesty, propriety; sense of honor

rēx, rēgis	king
sanguis, -inis	blood 50
sapiens, sapientis	sage, philosopher, wise/virtuous man; a teacher of wisdom
senātor, -tōris	senator
sermō, -ōnis	conversation, discussion; diction; talk; word
sōl, sōlis	sun
terror, -ōris	fright, terror, panic
timor, -ōris	fear, apprehension
vertex (or vortex), -icis	whirl; top of a whirl; summit, head, height
vetus, -eris	antiquity; (Pl) ancient times; traditional ways; forefathers; as adj: old, of long standing
victor, -ōris	conqueror

III. Feminine (--, -is)   [75 nouns]

	NOM	ACC	GEN	DAT	ABL
Sing	--	-em	-is	-ī	-e
Plur	-ēs	-ēs	-(i)um*	-ibus	-ibus

*The -i- of the Gen Pl ending is unpredictable and may or may not appear in any given word. There is no simple rule that will guarantee success in this matter.

aetās, -ātis	age, time of life
arbor, -oris	tree
ars, artis	skill, art
arx, arcis	citadel, castle; summit
auctoritas -tatis	authority, power; counsel, advice, encouragement
auris, -is	ear
avis, -is	bird
caedēs, -is	a cutting off; slaughter; gore
cīvitās, -ātis	community, city; citizens; rights, citizenship

13

clādēs, -is	destruction, slaughter
classis, -is	class, division; fleet
cōgitātiō, -ōnis	meditation, thinking
cohors, -tis	cohort, band; troop; yard, pen; crew of a ship; attendants, staff
cupiditas -tatis	enthusiasm, passion; carnal desire, lust; greed, usury; ambition
cupīdō, -inis	desire, eagerness, craving (often personified)
dīgnitās, -ātis	worth, rank, reputation, esteem, &c.
famēs, -is	hunger, famine
fax, facis	torch
frōns, frontis	forehead, brow; front of a place
frūx, frūgis	fruit of any kind
gēns, gentis	family, tribe, race
hiem(p)s, hiemis	winter
imāgō, -inis	image, form, figure, &c.
laus, -dis	praise
legiō, -ōnis	legion
lēx, lēgis	law, statute, ordinance (made by Senate and People)
lībertās, -ātis	freedom, liberty
libido libidinis	desire, longing; lust, wantonness; passion, lusts (Pl)
lūx, lūcis	light (of day)
magnitūdō, -īnis	greatness, size
māter, -tris	mother
mēns, mentis	mind (the rational faculty)
messis, -is	a mowing, reaping, or ingathering of the corn, &c.; harvest; the harvested crops; harvest-time
mōlēs, -is	lage mass; heap, pile; boulder; jetty, dam, dike; a monster
mors, -tis	death
mulier, -eris	woman (esp. married woman)
multitūdō, -inis	crowd, multitude; number, amount, body, a force; rabble, mob
nāvis, -is	ship

nix, nivis	snow (Gn Pl -ium)
nox, noctis	night
nūbēs, -is	cloud, storm cloud; crowd, throng
ops, opis	assistance, aid; (Pl) means, resources
ōrātiō, -ōnis	a pleading, speech, address
pars, partis	part
pāx, pācis	peace
pecus, -udis	cattle; sheep
pietās, -ātis	sense of duty, devotion, esp. between parents and children
plebes, plēbis	common people, general citizens; lower class; mob, the masses; *smtms:* plēbēs, plēbēī
potestās, -ātis	authority, just power
prex, precis	request, prayer (most freq. found in the Pl) 50
prōlēs, -is	offspring, descendants
quies quietis	quiet, calm, rest, peace; sleep
ratiō, -ōnis	a thinking, reckoning; method, way; reasoning; account, invoice; system or plan; consideration or reason
ratis, -is	raft; vessel
regiō, -ōnis	direction, line; boundary, limit; district, region
religiō, -ōnis	scruples; supernatural constraint, taboo; obligation; sanction; worship; rite; sanctity
salūs, -ūtis	health; prosperity; greeting; salvation, safety
sēdēs, -is	seat; abode, habitation; (Gn Pl -um)
senectūs, -ūtis	old age
soror, -ōris	sister
sors, sortis	lot; fate, destiny, oracle; success
tellūs, -ūris	Earth
tempestas -tātis	storm; season, time, weather
urbs, urbis	city
uxor, -ōris	wife
vestis, -is	grament, clothes; blanket; robe
vetustās, -ātis	age; old age; antiquity; long duration

vicis, vicis	turn, change, succession; exchange, repayment; plight, lot
virgō, -inis	
virtūs, -ūtis	manliness, valor, courage; virtues
vis, vīs (defective)	force, strength, energy; (sg. vis,vīs,vim,vī,vī; (Pl) virēs, virēs, virium viribus, viribus)
volucris, -is	bird; as adj., volucer, -cris, -cre: flying, winged
voluntās, -ātis	wish, desire
voluptās, -ātis	pleasure, enjoyment
vōx, vōcis	voice; utterance, word

III. Masculine/Femine (--, -is)   [14 nouns]

The following nouns may be M or F, depending on context.

	NOM	ACC	GEN	DAT	ABL
Sing	--	-em	**-is**	-ī	-e
Plur	-ēs	-ēs	-(i)um*	-ibus	-ibus

*The -i- of the Gen Pl ending is unpredictable and may or may not appear in any given word. Only long acquaintance with the individual terms will guarantee success in this matter.

adulēscēns, -entis	a youth, young man; young woman, maiden
anguis, -is	serpent, snake
auctor, -ōris	originator, producer, founder
bōs, bovis	ox; (Gn Pl boum; Dt/Ab Pl bōbus/būbus)
canis, -is	dog; (Ab S -e, Gn Pl canum)
cīvis, -is	citizen, fellow citizen
comes, -itis	comrade, companion
coniūnx (coniux), -iugis	consort, spouse, husband or wife
custōs, -ōdis	guard, watchman
hostis, -is	enemy; stranger, foreigner

iuvenis, -is	a youth, young man or woman; Gn Pl takes -*um*
parēns, -entis	parent (used for either father or mother)
senex, -is	an old man; *smtms:* old woman
vātēs, -is	prophet, soothsayer, seer, bard

III. Neuter (--, -is)   *[42 nouns]*

	NOM	ACC	GEN	DAT	ABL
Sing	--	--	-is	-ī	-e
Plur	-a	-a	-um	-ibus	-ibus

aequor, -oris	surface of the sea; any level smooth surface; a plain; the sea
aes, aeris	copper, bronze; anything made of bronze
agmen, -inis	line of march; army on the march
animal, -malis	animal; creature, beast; insect
caput, -itis	head
carmen, -inis	song
cor, cordis	heart
corpus, -oris	body
crīmen, -inis	verdict, decision; charge, accusation
decus, -oris	glory, honor; deeds; dignity, decorum, beauty
facinus, -noris	crime; outrange
flūmen, -inis	stream, river
frīgus, -oris	cold
fulmen, -inis	lightning; thunderbolt
fūnus, -eris	funeral; death, dead body, pyre
genus, -eris	birth, origin, lineage; offspring; tribe, people; sort, kind, &c.
iter, itineris	journey, route, line of march
iūs, iūris	right, law
latus, -teris	side, flank

līmen, -inis	threshold, lintel; door, house; smtms: barrier at a race
lītus, -oris	beach, shore
lūmen, -inis	a light
mare, -is	sea (AbS: mari; GnP: marium)
mīlia, -ium (Pl)	thousands; as adj., mīlle (indecl.)
moenia, -ium (Pl)	walls, fortifications
mūnus, -eris	task, function, service; gift, offering; bribe
nemus, -oris	open wood, glade; grove, forest; pasture
nōmen, -inis	name; (lit.) means of knowing
nūmen, -inis	divine help; divine glory; deity
opus, -eris	work
os, ossis	bone; kernal (nut); heartwood; pit or stone (fruit)
ōs, ōris	mouth; face; (Pl sometimes) speech
pectus, -oris	breast, bosom, chest; heart, soul, courage
pecus, -oris	cattle (general expression for the larger variety of domestic animals)
pondus, -eris	weight (both lit. and fig.)
rūs, rūris	country; (Pl) lands, fields
scelus, -eris	wicked deed, crime, sin
sēmen, -inis	seed (both lit. and fig.)
sīdus, -eris	star; constellation; *smtms:* weather (when Pl)
tempus, -oris	time; temple (beside the forehead)
vēr, vēris	spring
vulnus, -eris	wound

FOURTH DECLENSION

Masculine (-us, -ūs)   *[25 nouns]*

	NOM	ACC	GEN	DAT	ABL
Sing	**-us**	-um	**-ūs**	-uī	-ū
Plur	-ūs	-ūs	-uum	-ibus	-ibus

affectus, -ūs	affection, passion; goodwill;disposition, feeling; (Pl) loved ones
arcus, -ūs	bow; arch; (usually takes -ubus in the Dt and Ab Pl)
cantus, -ūs	song, music
cāsus, -ūs	a falling, fall; chance, accident
cultus, -ūs	cultivation, care, tending; training, education, refinement; reverence
currus, -ūs	chariot
cursus, -ūs	running; speed, zeal; charge; march; revolving (wheel); an advance
exercitus, -ūs	training; army
flūctus, -ūs	wave, flood; tumult, disorder
frūctus, -ūs	fruit; produce; benefit, enjoyment
gradus, gradus	step; position
impetus, -ūs	charge, attack, rush
lacus, -ūs	lake (*smtms* takes -ubus in Dt and AbPl)
mānēs, -ium (Pl)	deifiied souls of the dead; ghosts, shades; gods of the Lower Word
metus, -ūs	fear, apprehension, dread
motus, motus	motion, movement; riot, disturbance; gesture; emotion
portus, -ūs	port, harbor (*smtms* takes -ubus in Dt and Ab Pl)
senātus, -ūs	council of elders, senate
sēnsus, -ūs	feeling, emotion, sense
sinus, -ūs	fold; bosom of a robe; gulf, bay

spīritus, -ūs	breathing, breath; breath of life, life; high spirit, pride, courage
tumultus, -ūs	commotion, uprising
ūsus, -ūs	use, advantage; experience; ūsus est: it is necessary (+Ab)
versus, -ūs	rank, tier; verse; a turning
vultus, -ūs	expression; face

IV. Feminine (-us -ūs)   [3 nouns]

	NOM	ACC	GEN	DAT	ABL
Sing	**-us**	-um	**-ūs**	-uī*	-ū*
Plur	-ūs	-ūs	-uum	-ibus	-ibus

* Fem nouns of the IV Dcl sometimes took -ō as the Dat or Abl S.

domus, -ūs	home, house (Dt S: domō; Ac Pl: domōs)
laurus, -ūs	bay-tree, laurel; wreath of laurel
manus, -ūs	hand; crowd, group; band, a force

IV. Neuter (-ū -ūs)   [1 noun]

	NOM	ACC	GEN	DAT	ABL
Sing	**-ū**	-ū	**-ūs**	-ū	-ū
Plur	-ua	-ua	-uum	-ibus	-ibus

cornū, -ūs	horn; beak; bow; trumpet; mountain peak; anything shaped like a horn

FIFTH DECLENSION

	NOM	ACC	GEN	DAT	ABL
Sing	-ēs	-em	-ēī	-ēī	-ē
Plur	-ēs	-ēs	-ērum	-ēbus	-ēbus

Masculine -ēs -ēī   *[1 noun]*

diēs, -ēī	day; *smtms:* F, when referencing a fixed day or period of time

Feminine -ēs -ēī   *[8 nouns]*

aciēs, -ēī	edge; front or line of battle
faciēs, -ēī	form, figure, appearance; face
fidēs, -eī	trust, faith; pledge, reliability, protection
plebes, -ei	common people, general citizens; lower class; mob, the masses; *smtms:* plebes, plēbis
rēs, reī	thing
respublica	res + publicus -a -um (adj) used as a substantive
speciēs, -ēī	aspect, appearance
spēs, -eī	hope

INDECLINABLE NOUNS

fās	divine right or law; + inf., permissible to
nefās	anything contrary to divine law; impiety, wickedness; sin, abomination
nihil or nīl	nothing; no; nonsense

VERBS

Verbs occur in four conjugations. Of the 1,325 most common words in Classical Latin, 413 (about 31%) are verbs. The student will find them distributed as follows:

CONJUGATION		DEP/SEMI	TOTAL
First	91	8	99
Second	66	7	73
Third	141	16	157
Fourth	19	2	21
Mixed III/IV	24		24
Iregular	39		39
Totals	380	33	413

FIRST CONJUGATION

	SING	PLURAL
1	-ō	-ā-mus
2	-ā-s	-ā-tis
3	-a-t	-a-nt
Inf	**-āre**	

Regular   *[91 verbs]*

aedificō, -āre, -āvī, -ātus	to build
aestimō, -āre, -āvī, -ātus	to value, assess; estimate; judge
agitō, -āre, -āvī, -ātus	to drive (esp. of hunters), to hound; to brandish
ambulo, -āre, -āvī, -ātus	to walk
amō, -āre, -āvī, -ātus	to love
appellō, -āre, -āvī, -ātus	to accost, call, call upon
appropinquō, -āre, -āvī, -ātus	to approach, come near to
armō, -āre, -āvī, -ātus	to arm, equip
cantō, -āre, -āvī, -ātus	to sing; play on an instrument
celebrō, -āre, -āvī, -ātus	to frequent, throng, crowd; celebrate, extol
celō, -āre, -āvī, -ātus	to hide, conceal
certō, -āre, -āvī, -ātus	to make certain, decide (by contest); fight, contend, compete
cessō, -āre, -āvī, -ātus	to move back; be idle, delay, loiter, hesitate; cease
circumdō, -dare, -dedī, -datus	to put around
citō, -āre, -āvī, citātus	to urge on, encourage
cōgitō, -āre, -āvī, -ātus	to reflect, consider, think, draw together
clamō, -āre, -āvī, -ātus	to shout
comparō, -āre, -āvī, -ātus	to get ready, provide; compare

cōnstō, -stāre, -stitī, -statūrus	to stand with, agree, be consistent with; be complete, regular; cost; it is established, certain
creō, -āre, -āvī, -ātus	to bring forth, produce, create; elect
cūrō, -āre, -āvī, -ātus	to care for; provide for; care to
damnō, -āre, -āvī, -ātus	to inflict loss; declare guilty, condemn
dō, dāre, dedī, datus	to give, put (latter meaning rare except in compounds)
dōnō, -āre, -āvī, -ātus	to give, present as a gift
dubitō, -āre, -āvī, -ātus	to doubt; deliberate; hesitate
errō, -āre, -āvī, -ātus	to go astray, wander; err
exīstimō, -āre, -āvī, -ātus	to form an opinion of; think; suppose
exspectō, -āre, -āvī, -ātus	to look out; watch, wait, expect
festīnō, -āre, -āvī, -ātus	to hurry
habitō, -āre, -āvī, -ātus	to dwell, live
iactō, -āre, -āvī, -ātus	to throw often, fling, toss; bandy words, vaunt
imperō, -āre, -āvī, -ātus	to command; control
indicō, -āre, -āvī, -ātus	to point out, show, make known, &c.; (rarely) betray, accuse
īnstō, -stāre, -stitī, -statūrus	to follow; persist; labor at; menace; be at hand
intrō, -āre, -āvī, -ātus	to enter; penetrate
iūrō, -āre, -āvī, -ātus	to take an oath, swear
iuvō, -āre, iūvī, iūtus	to help, aid, assist; please, delight
invītō, -āre, -āvī, -ātus	to invite
labōrō, -āre, -āvī, -ātus	to work, produce
lacrimō, -āre, -āvī, -ātus	to weep
laudō, -āre, -āvī, -ātus	to praise
levō, -āre, -āvī, -ātus	to lift; remove; lessen, relieve; make light
liberō, -āre, -āvī, -ātus	to free, set loose
locō, -āre, -āvī, -ātus	to place, locate; lend at interest
mandō, -āre, -āvī, -ātus	to hand over, commission
memorō, -āre, -āvī, -ātus	to recall, recount, relate
mūtō, -āre, -āvī, -ātus	to change

narrō, -āre, -āvī, -ātus	to relate, recount, narrate
nāvigō, -āre, -āvī, -ātus	to sail
necō, -āre, -āvī, -ātus	to kill, murder 50
negō, -āre, -āvī, -ātus	to say no, deny, refuse
notō, -āre, -āvī, notātus	to note, mark out, watch, notice
numerō, -āre, -āvī, -ātus	to count, reckon, number; pay, count out pay; number as one's own, have
nuntiō, -āre, -āvī, -ātus	to announce
occupō, -āre, -āvī, -ātus	to seize; overtake; capture, occupy; attack
offerō, -āre, -āvī, -ātus	to offer; present; bestow
oppugnō, -āre, -āvī, -ātus	to attack
optō, -āre, -āvī, -ātus	to choose, select; wish, desire
ōrnō, -āre, -āvī, -ātus	to fit out, equip; embellish, adorn
ōrō, -āre, -āvī, -ātus	to beg
parō, -āre, -āvī, -ātus	to prepare, get ready; acquire
penetrō, -āre, -āvī, -ātus	to penetrate, react
poenas do	to pay the penalty; am punsihed
portō, -āre, -āvī, -ātus	to carry
praestō, -stāre, -stitī, -stitus	to stand in front, excel; exhibit, furnish
probō, -āre, -āvī, -ātus	to find good, approve; prove
properō, -āre, -āvī, -ātus	to hasten, speed
pūgnō, -āre, -āvī, -ātus	to fight
putō, -āre, -āvī, -ātus	to arrange, set in order; reckon, think; trim, clean
rēgnō, -āre, -āvī, -ātus	to reign
revocō, -āre, -āvī, -ātus	to call back, recall (lit. & fig.)
rogō, -āre, -āvī, -ātus	to ask, beg, request
salūtō, -āre, -āvī, -ātus	to greet
servō, -āre, -āvī, -ātus	to save; keep, guard, watch over, protect
sonō, -āre, -nuī, -nitus	to sound, resound
spectō, -āre, -āvī, -ātus	to look, face, look at, consider
spērō, -āre, -āvī, -ātus	to hope

spīrō, -āre, -āvī, -ātus	to breathe, blow
stō, stāre, stetī, status	to stand
superō, -āre, -āvī, -ātus	to overcome, surpass, defeat
temperō, -āre, -āvī, -ātus	to divide or combine duly; to regulate, adjust; to qualify, temer, restrain, abstain
temptō, -āre, -āvī, -ātus	to try, test; attempt
tentō, -āre, -āvī, -ātus	to handle, feel; try; prove; attack
vacō, -āre, -āvī, -ātus	to be empty, open, unoccupied; be idle, free from.
versō, -āre, -āvī, -ātus	to turn often, keep turning, wind; (pass.) move, be busy; dwell; conduct one's self
vigilō, -āre, -āvī, -ātus	to be awake, be on guard
vītō, -āre, -āvī, -ātus	to avoid, shun
vocō, -āre, -āvī, -ātus	to call, name
volō, -āre, -āvī, -ātus	to fly
vulgō, -āre, -āvī, -ātus	to spread among the multitude; make general, common; make known to all by words; publish
vulnerō, -āre, -āvī, -ātus	wound, injure

I. Deponent [8 verbs]

arbitror, -ārī, -ātus sum	to serve as referee; consider; think, hold, deem
cōnor, -ārī, -ātus sum	to attempt, try
fruor, fruī, frūctus sum	to enjoy
hortor, -ārī, -ātus sum	to encourage, urge on
imitor, -ārī, -ātus sum	to imitate
mīror, -ārī, -ātus sum	to wonder at, marvel at
moror, -āri, -ātus sum	to delay
precor, -ārī, -ātus sum	to pray, supplicate, invoke

SECOND CONJUGATION

	SING	PLURAL
1	-e-ō	-ē-mus
2	-ē-s	-ē-tis
3	-e-t	-e-nt
Inf	**-ēre**	

Regular   *[66 verbs]*

appareō, -ēre, āruī, -itus	to appear; be evident, noticed; show up, occur
ārdeō, -ēre, ārsī, ārsus	to burn; glow; be inflamed with desire
augeō, -ēre, auxī, auctus	to increase; exalt
careō, -ēre, -uī, -itūrus	to be without, want
caveō, -ēre, cāvī, cautus	to be on one's guard, beware
cēnseō, -ēre, -suī, -sus	to assess, rate, estimate; propose, determine, decide, think
contineō, -ēre, -tinuī, -tentus	to hold together; contain; bound, limit, restrain, &c. in many senses
dēbeō, -ēre, -uī, -itus	to owe to; be obliged to; (lit.) have from
decet, -ēre, decuit, --	it becomes, behooves (*impers*)
dēleō, -ēre, -evī, -etus	to destroy
doceō, -ēre, docuī, doctus	to teach; inform
doleō, -ēre, doluī, dolitūs	to feel pain; grieve
egeō, -ēre, -uī, --	to be destitute, lack
exerceō, -ēre, -uī, -itus	to keep on; keep busy; to work at; oversee
faveō, -ēre, fāvī, fautus	to favor
fleō, -ēre, -ēvī, -ētus	to weep
flōreō, -ēre, -uī, --	to bloom
fulgeō, -ēre, fulsī, --	to shine brightly, gleam, flash

habeō, -ēre, -uī, -itus	to have, hold, possess, cherish, contain, occupy, deem
haereō, haerēre, haesi, haesus	to stick, adhere, cling to; hesitate; be in difficulties
horreō, -ēre, -uī, --	to bristle; bristle at, shudder at
iaceō, -ēre, -uī, -itus	to lie down; lie ill, in ruins; sleep
impleō, -ēre, -ēvī, -ētus	to fill in, fill up
invideō, -ēre, -vīdī, -vīsus	to look on, envy
iubeō, -ēre, iussī, iussus	to bid, order
lateō, -ēre, -uī, --	to lie hid, be hidden; (with Ac. of person in poetry) be hid from, unknown
libet, -ēre, libuit, libitua	it pleases (*impers*)
licet, -ēre, -uit, licitus	it is permitted (*impers*)
lūceō, -ēre, lūxī, --	to be light, gleam, shine
maereō, -ēre, -uī, --	to grieve, mourn
maneō, -ēre, mānsī, mānsus	to remain, abide
mereō, -ēre, -uī, -itus	to deserve, merit; serve (as a soldier)
misceō, -ēre, miscuī, mixtus	to mix, mingle
moneō, -ēre, -uī, -itus	to warn, advise
moveō, -ēre, mōvī, mōtus	to move (lit. & fig.)
niteō, -ēre, -uī, --	to shine, glitter, gleam
noceō, -ēre, -uī, -itus	to harm
oportet, -tēre, -tuit, --	it behooves, ought to (*impers*)
palleō, -ēre, -uī, --	to be/look ash-coloured, wan, pale
pareō, -ēre, parui, partitus	to obey (+ Dt)
pateō, -ēre, -uī, --	to lie open, extend, spread
pendeō, -ēre, pependī, --	to hang, be suspended (lit. & fig.)
persuādeō, -ēre, -suasi, persuasus	to persuade (+ Dt)
pertineō, -ēre, -tinuī, --	to extend through; lead to, pertain to, bear upon
placeō, -ēre, -uī, -itus	to please

praebeō, -ēre, -buī, -bitus	to afford, furnish; hold in front
prōcēdō, -ēre, -cessī, -cessus	to go forth, advance
prohibeō, -ēre, -uī, -itus	to hold forward; keep away, restrain
pudeō, -ēre, -uī, -itus	to make ashamed, put to shame; *smtms:* pudet, -ere
respondeō, -ēre, -ondī, -ōnsus	to reply, make answer; pledge in return ₅₀
retineō, -ēre, -tinuī, retentus	to hold back, detain; maintain, keep
rīdeō, -ēre, rīsī, rīsus	to laugh, laugh at
rubeō, -ēre, -uī, --	to grow red, redden, blush, colour up
sedeō, -ēre, sēdī, sessus	to sit; be fixed, settled; *smtms:* to fit, suit
sileō, -ēre, -uī, --	to be/keep quiet, still, silent, &c.
sustineō, -ēre, sustinuī, sustentus	to hold under, i.e. hold up, sustain
taceō, -ēre, -uī, -itus	to be silent
teneō, -ēre, tenuī, tentus	to hold, keep; to grasp; comprehend
terreō, -ēre, -uī, -itus	to terrify, frighten
timeō, -ēre, -uī, --	to fear, dread
torqueō, -ēre, torsi, tortus	to turn, twist; hurl; torture; bend, distort; spin
torreō, -ēre, torruī, tostus	to parch, scorch; (of a stream) rush
urgeō, -ēre, ursī, --	to drive, impel, press hard, urge
valeō, -ēre, -uī, -itūrus	to be strong (physically); (fig.) excel, be able, have power, be worth
videō, -ēre, vīdī, vīsus	to see; (Ps) appear, seem, be seen
vireō, -ēre, -uī, --	to be verdant, green; be lively, vigorous

II. Deponent/Semideponent [7 verbs]

fateor, fateri, fassus sum	to admit, confess; disclose, praise (+ Dt)
reor, rērī, ratus sum	to reckon, calculate; think
tueor, -ērī, tuitus (tūtus) sum	to look at; protect

vereor, -ērī, veritus sum	to fear, stand in awe of
audeō, -ēre, ausus sum	to be eager; dare, venture (semi- dep)
gaudeō, -ēre, gāvīsus sum	to rejoice (semi-dep)
soleō, -ēre, solitus sum	to be accustomed (semi-dep)

THIRD CONJUGATION

	SING	PLURAL
1	-ō	-i-mus
2	-i-s	-i-tis
3	-i-t	-u-nt
Inf	-ēre	

Regular [141 verbs]

accēdō, -ere, accessī, accessus	to approach; to assent; to be added to (as pass. of addo); increase, wax
accidō, -ere, -cidī, --	to fall to; happen, suffer, experience (usu. in a bad sense)
addō, -ere, -didī, -ditus	to give to, add; add
agō, -ere, ēgī, āctus	to drive, carry on, do, act; treat, discuss; (of time) spend
alō, -ere, aluī, alitus	to nourish, feed; strengthen, sustain
āmittō, -ere, -mīsī, -missus	to let go away, lose; send away, dismiss
ascendō, -ere, ī, ascensus	to climb
bibō, -ere, bibī, --	to drink
cadō, -ere, cecidī, cāsūrus	to fall; *smtms*: be slain
caedō, -ere, caecidī, caesus	to chop, hew, cut down; strike, murder; slaughter; sodomize
canō, -ere, cecinī, cantus	to sing
carpō, -ere, carpsī, carptus	to pluck

cēdō, -ere, cessī, cessus	to move, step; go away; yield, retreat
cernō, -ere, crēvī, crētus	to see, make out; sift, discern, distinguish; examine; decide; separate, sift (rare)
cingō, -ere, cinxī, cinctus	to encircle, surround, gird
claudō, -ere, clausī, clausus	to close, shut
cognōscō, -ere, -gnōvī, -gnitus	to become acquainted with; recognize understand, learn; know (esp. in Prf); examine (legal)
cōgō, -ere, coēgī, coāctus	to drive together; gather; force, compel
colligō, -ere, -lēgī, -lēctus	to collect; assemble; harvest; pick up
colō, -ere, coluī, cultus	to till, cultivate; dwell in; cultivate, cherish, worship
committō, -ere, -mīsī, -missus	to join together; entrust; perform, do, allow
compōnō, -ere, -posuī, -positus	to put together; build, construct, arrange; adjust, quiet, appease; bury, lay away
concēdō, -ēre, -cessī, -cessus	to go with; retire, withdraw; yield, submit; smtms: forgive
condō, -ere, -didī, -ditus	to put together, form; build, found; compose; store up; conceal
consistō, -ere, constitī, constitus	to stop, halt; linger; take up a position
cōnstituō, -ere, -uī, -ūtus	to put together, establish, set up, station; determine
cōnsulō, -ere, -luī, -ltus	to plan, deliberate consult; take thought for
cōnsūmō, -ere, -sūmpsī, -sūmptus	to eat, eat up, devour
contemnō, -ere, contempsī, -ptus	to despise, scorn, disdain
contingō, -ere, -tigī, -tāctus	to touch, be contiguous to; happen to
convertō, -ere, vertī, -versus	to turn about, turn, change
corrumpō, -ere, -rūpī, -ruptus	to break up, destroy, ruin, spoil, &c.
crēdō, -ere, -didī, -ditus	to believe, trust
crēscō, -ere, crēvī, crētus	to grow, increase
currō, -ere, cucurrī, cursus	to run

decernō -ere decrevī decretus	to decide, determine, resolve; decree; judge; vote for
dēdūco, -ere, -dūxī, -ductus	to lead away; (of ships) launch; lead, bring into
dēfendō, -ere, -endī, -ēnsus	to thrust off, ward off, defend
deligo, -ere, -ī, delectus	to pick off, cull; choose, enroll; conduct a levy
dēscendō, -ere, -scendī, -scēnsus	to climb down, descend
dēserō, -ere, -seruī, -sertus	to disjoin, leave off, give up, abandon
dēsinō, -ere, siī, situs	to leave off, cease, forbear
dētrahō, -ere, -trāxī, -tractus	to draw off, pull off, rob
dīcō, -ere, dīxī, dictus	to say, state, speak
dīligō, -ere, -lēxī, -lēctus	to choose, pick out; love, cherish
dīmittō, -ere, -mīsī, -missus	to send apart, send away, dismiss, let go
discēdō, -ere, -cessī, -cessus	to depart; to divide, separate
discō, -ere, didicī, discitus	to learn
dīvidō, -ere, -vīsī, -vīsus	to divide, separate
dūcō, -ere, dūxī, ductus	to lead; deem, consider, hold 50
ēdūcō, -ere, -dūxī, -ductus	to bring up, rear, educate, lead
effundō, -ere, -fūdī, -fūsus	to pour out, pour forth
emō, -ere, -emī, -emptus	to buy
ēvādō, -ere, -vāsī, -vāsum	evade, escape; avoid
exigō, -ere, -egī, exactus	to drive out, expel; examine, weigh
exstinguō, -ere, -stinxī, -stinctus	to quench, extinguish; kill; destroy
fallō, -ere, fefellī, falsus	to deceive, violate, betray; escape notice; dēceptus often serves as Prf Ps Participle
fīgō, -ere, fīxī, fīxus	to fix, fasten; set up, establish; transfix, shoot
fingō, -ere, fīnxī, fictus	to shape; invent; think
flectō, -ere, flexī, flexus	to bend, turn
fluō, -ere, flūxī, flūxus	to flow

32

frangō, -ere, frēgī, frāctus	to break, shatter
fundō, -ere, fūdī, fūsus	to pour; scatter, disperse, rout
gerō, gerere, gessī, gestus	to bear, carry; carry on, accomplish, manage
gignō, -ere, genuī, genitus	to beget; bear, bring forth
impellō, -ere, -pulī, -pulsus	to drive on, impel; excite, urge on
impōnō, -ere, -posuī, -positus	to put upon; impose, levy upon; put in
incendō, -ere, -dī, -incensus	to burn, set afire
īnferō, īnferre, intulī, illātus	to bear in, upon, come against; attack in war
īnstituō, -ere, -uī, -ūtus	to set up, set on, establish, undertake; equip
intellegō, -ere, -lēxī, lēctus	to pick out from between; understand, be aware
intendō, -ere, -tendī, -tentus	to stretch out, strain; *smtms*: determine (+ inf.)
iungō, -ere, iūnxī, iūnctus	to join
laedō, -ere, laesī, laesus	to injure by striking, hurt
legō, -ere, lēgī, lēctus	to gather, collect; weigh anchor; read; pick, choose
linquō, -ere, līquī, lictus	to leave, quit, forsake; abandon, desist; bequeath
lūdō, -ere, lūsī, lūsus	to play; make sport of
metuō, -ere, -uī, --	to fear, apprehend, dread
mittō, -ere, mīsī, missus	to send, let go
nectō, -ere, nex(u)ī, nexus	to bind, unite
negligō, -ere, -lēxī, lēctus	to disregard, neglect; ignore; despise
nōscō, -ere, nōvī, nōtus	to come to know; (Prf.) know
nūbō, -ere, nūpsī, nuptus	to marry; to veil for the marriage ceremony
occīdō, -ere, -cīdī, -cīsus	to cut down, kill
occurrō, -ere, occucurrī, occursus	to run to meet; oppose, resist; come to mind, occur (+ Dt)
omittō, -ere, omisī, omissus	to omit; let go; disregard
opprimō, -ere, -pressī, -pressus	to press against; crush, overwhelm; surprise

ostendō, -ere, -tendī, -tensus	to stretch towards, hold out; expose to view, show
pandō, -ere, pandī, passus	to spread, spread out; expand
parcō, -ere, parcuī, parsūs	to spare, be sparing of
pellō, -ere, pepulī, pulsus	to strike, beat, push, drive
pendō, -ere, pependī, pēnsus	to weigh, hang, suspend; pay
peragō, -ere, -ēgī, -āctus	to drive through; finish; accomplish
perdō, -ere, -didī, -ditus	to destroy, loose; put through
permittō, -ere, -mīsī, -missus	allow to go through; to cut loose; to give up, entrust, commit; let fly, cast hurl; to yield, allow, permit
petō, -ere, -īvī (-iī), -ītus	to fall upon, attack; aim at; seek, demand, ask for
pingō, -ere, pīnxī, pictus	to paint; embroider; ornament; decorate
plaudō, -ere, plausī, plausus	to beat; flatter, clap
pōnō, -ere, posuī, positus	to put, put down, place, establish
poscō, -ere, poposcī, --	to ask, demand 100
praecipiō, -cipere, -cepī, -ceptus	to receive in advance; anticipate; warn; teach, instruct
premō, -ere, pressī, pressus	to press, press hard, pursue, overwhelm, &c.
prōdō, -ere, -didī, -ditus	to give forth, publish, hand down; give over, betray
prōiciō, -ere, -iēcī, -iectus	to throw forward/forth, hurl; renounce
prōmittō, -ere, -mīsī, -missus	to permit to grow; proffer; promise, agree; let go forth
prōpōnō, -ere, -posuī, -positus	to put forward, set forth, propose, present, &c.
quaerō, -ere, -sīvī, -sītus	to search, seek; ask, inquire
quatiō, -ere, --, quassus	to shake
quiēscō, -ere, -ēvī, -ētus	to go to rest; keep quiet, esp. sleep
reddō, -ere, -didī, -ditus	to give back, return; render
regō, -ere, rēxī, rēctus	to guide, direct; esp. rule
relinquō, -ere, -līquī, -lictus	to leave behind, abandon
repetō, -ere, -īvī (-iī), -ītus	to seek back, demand, exact; revisit; call to mind, recollect; repeat

resistō, -ere, restiti, --	to resist
revertō, -ere, -i, --	to turn back; return; recur
rumpō, -ere, rupi, ruptus	to burst
ruō, -ere, ruī, rutus	to overthrow, throw down; rush down, tumble down
scrībō, -ere, scrīpsī, scrīptus	to write
sinō, -ere, sīvī, situs	to let go, allow, permit, suffer
solvō, -ere, solvī, solūtus	to loosen, release; set sail; perform, pay, fulfill
spargō, -ere, -rsī, -rsus	to scatter
spernō, -ere, sprēvī, sprētus	to reject, despise, scorn; sever, remove
statuō, -ere, -uī, -ūtus	to set up, station, fix; resolve, determine
sternō, -ere, strāvī, strātus	to strew, spread out, stretch out; overthrow; devastate
sūmō, -ere, sūmpsī, sūmptus	to take up, take
surgō, -ere, surrēxī, surrēctus	to raise; rise
tangō, -ere, tetigī, tāctus	to touch
tegō, -ere, tēxī, tēctus	to cover; conceal
tendō, -ere, tetendī, tentus	to stretch
terō, -ere, trīvī, trītus	to rub
tollō, -ere, sustulī, sublātus	to raise up, exalt; acknowledge; weigh anchor;
trādō, -ere, -didī, -ditus	to give over, hand over; entrust, yield
trahō, -ere, trāxī, tractus	to drag, draw, draw in
tribuō, -ere, -uī, -ūtus	to assign, bestow, grant, &c.
ūrō, -ere, ussī, ustus	to burn
vehō, -ere, vēxī, vectus	to carry; (Ps.) ride, go, sail,
vendō, -ere, vendidi, venditus	to sell
vertō, -ere, -rtī, -rsus	to turn; (Ps.) revolve
vincō, -ere, vīcī, victus	to conquer, vanquish
vīvō, -ere, vīxī, vīctūrus	to live, subsist
volvō, -ere, volvī, volūtus	to roll, twist; turn over, revolve

III. Deponent   [16 verbs]

complector, -ī, complexus sum	to entwine with, embrace, surround
cōnsequor, -ī, -secūtus sum	to follow up, overtake, attain
ēgridior, -ī, egressus sum	to go out
ingredior, -ī, ingressus sum	to enter
īrāscor, -ī, iratus sum	to get angry
lābor, lābī, lāpsus sum	to glide, slip, slide
loquor, -ī, locūtus sum	to speak, talk
morior, morī, mortuus sum	to die
nāscor, -ī, nātus sum	to be born (with many fig. uses)
orior, orīrī, ortus sum	to arise; spring from, begin
patior, -ī, passus sum	to permit, endure
proficiscor, proficiscī, profectus sum	to depart, set out; proceed
queror, -ī, questus sum	to complain of, lament
regredior, regredī, regressus sum	to go back, return
sequor, -ī, secūtus sum	to follow
ūtor, ūtī, ūsus sum	to use, employ (with Ab)

FOURTH CONJUGATION

	SING	PLURAL
1	-iō	-ī-mus
2	-ī-s	-ī-tis
3	-i-t	-iu-nt
Inf	**-īre**	

Regular [*19 verbs*]

adveniō, -ire, -i, -tus	to arrive
aperiō, -īre, -ruī, -rtus	to uncover, open
audiō, -īre, -īvī, -ītus	to hear, listen to
conveniō, -īre, -vēnī, -ventus	to come together, assemble; meet
custōdiō, -īre, -īvī, -ītus	to guard
dormiō, -īre, -īvī, -ītus	to sleep
ēveniō, -īre, -vēnī, -ventus	to come forth; happen
feriō, -īre, --, --	to hit, strike; kill, deliver the death blow; strike a deal; (for Prf, īcō or percūtiō is usu. used)
hauriō, -īre, hausī, haustus	to draw (any fluid); fig: to take
inveniō, -īre, -vēnī, -ventus	to come upon, find; (rarely) find out
nesciō, -īre, -īvī, -ītus	to not know, be ignorant
perveniō, -īre, -vēnī, -ventus	to get through, arrive, reach
pūniō, -īre, -iī, -itus	to punish
reperiō, -īre, repperī, repertus	to find out (after search)
sciō, scīre, scīvī (sciī), scītus	to know; know how
sentiō, -īre, sēnsī, sēnsus	to perceive by senses; feel, hear, see; perceive
serviō, -īre, -īvī, -ītus	to be a slave, serve
veniō, -īre, vēnī, ventus	to come
vinciō, -īre, vinxī, vinctus	to bind

IV. Deponent   *[2 verbs]*

exorior, -orīrī, -ortus sum	to rise up, appear, arise
experior, -īrī, expertus sum	to try thoroughly, test, experience

THIRD & FOURTH MIXED:
THIRD CONJ. VERBS IN -IO , [24 VERBS]

These verbs behave as regular III Conj verbs in the Inf and Perf tense; they take IV Conj forms in the Present, Future, and Imperfect.

	SING	PLURAL
1	-iō	-ī-mus
2	-ī-s	-ī-tis
3	-i-t	-iu-nt
Inf	**-ere**	

accipiō, -ere, -cēpī, -ceptus	to take to, i.e. receive, accept; suffer; learn
adiciō, -ere, -iēcī, -iectus	to add to, construct near to, be near to
afficiō, -ere, -fēcī, -fectus	to do to (a person); affect, visit with
aspiciō, -ere, -spexī, -spectus	to look to/at, behold
capiō, -ere, cēpī, captus	to take, seize
cōnficiō, -ere, -fēcī, -fectus	to make together; accomplish, complete; do up, exhaust
cōnspiciō, -ere, -spexī, -spectus	to catch sight of, behold
cupiō, -ere, -īvī, -ītus	to long for, crave, desire
dēficiō, -ere, -fēcī, -fectus	to make away from; fail, give out; revolt from

efficiō, -ere, -fēcī, -fectus	to work out, bring about, effect, complete; render
effugiō, -ere, -ūgī, -ūgitus	to escape
ēripiō, -ere, -ripuī, -reptus	to snatch away; save, rescue
excipiō, -ere, -cēpī, -ceptus	to take out, take up; to except, relieve
faciō, -ere, fēcī, factus	to do, make (in many senses and phrases)
fugiō, -ere, fūgī, fugitūrus	to flee, escape
iaciō, -ere, iēcī, iactus	to throw
incipiō, -ere, -cēpī, -ceptus	to take on, begin
interficiō, -ere, -fēcī, -fectus	to make away with, kill, put to death
obiciō, -ere, obiecī, obiectus	to throw before; object, oppose; upbraid
pariō, -ere, peperī, partus	to bring forth, give birth to, bear; accomplish, effect
rapiō, -ere, rapuī, raptus	to tear, seize, snatch
recipiō, -ere, -cēpī, -ceptus	to take back, receive esp. one's due; (loosely) receive
respiciō, -ere, -exī, -ectus	to look back, regard; give heed to, consider
trāiciō, -ere, -iēcī, -iectus	to throw across; pass over; pierce

IRREGULAR VERBS   [39 verbs]

āiō, --, --, --	I (you, he/she, they) affirm, maintain, say yes
coepī, coepisse, coeptus	to have begun; exists only in Prf, PluPrf, FutPrf, with incipio used as the Pr, Imprf, Fut
edō, -ere (or ēsse), ēdī, ēsus	to eat
eō, īre, iī (īvī), itus	to go
abeō, -īre, -iī, -itus	to go away, depart
adeō, -īre, -iī, -itus	to go to, visit; consult; undergo
exeo, exīre, exivī, exitus	to leave, go out from; perish, die
obeō, -īre, -iī (-īvī), -itus	to go toward, go to meet, traverse; enter upon, undergo; die
pereō, -īre, -iī, -itus	to go through; perish, be lost; also used as Ps of perdo
praetereō, -īre, -iī, -itus	to go by, pass, pass over
redeō, -īre, -iī, -itus	to go back, return
subeō, -īre, -iī, -itus	to go under, go up to; occur to; undergo, endure; (poetry) approach
trānseō, -īre, -iī, -itus	to go across, cross
ferō, ferre, tulī, lātum	to bear , carry, endure; declare
afferō, afferre, attulī, allātus	to bring to, carry to (usually fig. of reports, news); (of emotions) excite
auferō, -ferre, abstulī, ablātus	to bear away, bear off, take away, remove, &c.
cōnferō, -ferre, -tulī, collātus	to bring together, collect; bring to, transport; shift, transfer, compare
dēferō, -ferre, -tulī, -lātus	to bear away, carry away; report
differō, -erre, distulī, dīlātus	to bear apart, differ; postpone; spread apart
perferō, -ferre, -tulī, -lātus	to bear through, carry through; endure to the end; carry news, announce
praeferō, -ferre, -tulī, -lātus	to bear before; place before, prefer; hand to; show, reveal
referō, -ferre, -ttulī, -lātus	to bear back, bring back; report, refer, announce
fīō, fierī (fīerī), factus sum	to become (used as Pr Ps of facio).

fore	identical to futurum esse; forem -es -ent is Imprf Sbj used like essem, esses....
forem, -es, -et	Largely poetic form of essem
inquam, -quit, -quiunt, -quio, -quis	I say, he/she / it said, says; usu. placed after the first word or words of a quotation.
mālō, mālle, māluī, --	to wish for; prefer
nōlō, nōlle, nōluī, --	to be unwilling
volō, velle, voluī, --	to will, wish, be willing
meminī, -isse, --	to remember; pay heed; be sure; exists only in Prf, PluPrf, FutPrf, though *smtms* present in meaning
sum, esse, fuī, futūrus	to be, exist
absum, abesse, āfuī āfutūrus	to be away, be absent
adsum, -esse, -fuī, -futūrus	to be present, at hand, assist; *smtms:* assum, &c.
assum adesse affui affuturus	to be near, present, in attendance; arrive; assist, help (+Dt)
dēsum, -esse, -fuī, -futurus	to be lacking, missing
intersum, -esse, -fui, -futurus	to lie between, be in the midst; participate; be present
possum, posse, potuī, --	to be able, can
prōsum, -desse, -fuī, -futurus	to be profitable
supersum, -esse, -fuī, -futurus	to be over, remain, survive, &c.

Adjectives

Adjectives decline in a variety of patterns, often containing some variations even within the pattern; most of these variations are easily recognized. Of the 1,325 most common words in Latin, 243 (about 18%) are adjectives. The student will find them generally distributed as follows:

Declension	Note	Standard identification	No.
I & II (**2-1-2 endings**)	masc, neut decline like II Dcl nouns; fem decline like I Dcl	-us/-er, -a, -um	**173**
2-1-2 -ius	irregular 2-1-2 adjectives		**9**
III, 1 ending	one Nm ending covers all genders; lexicon also gives the Gen S	--, -is	**13**
III, 2 endings	one ending for masc & fem; separate ending for neut	-is, -e	**33**
III, 3 endings	separate endings for each gender	-er, -eris, -ere	**2**
Other	indeclinable, irregular, numeral, common comparison		**13**
Total:			**243**

2-1-2 ADJECTIVES
[I & II DECLENSION ADJECTIVES]

	Singular			Plural		
	M	**F**	**Nt**	**M**	**F**	**Nt**
Nm	**-us***	**-a**	**-um**	-ī	-ae	-a
Ac	-um	-am	-um	-ōs	–ās	-a
Gn	-ī	-ae	-ī	-ōrum	–ārum	-ōrum
Dt	-ō	-ae	-ō	-īs	-īs	-īs
Ab	-ō	–ā	-ō	-īs	-īs	-īs

*Some M adjectives end in -r or -er in the Nom S. As with the nouns, some of those ending in -er will keep the -e- as they decline while others will drop it.

Regular   *[173 adjectives]*

adversus, -a, -um	turned towards; facing, opposed; unfavorable
aeger, -gra, -grum	sick (body or soul)
aequus, -a, -um	level, even, equal; fair, kindly
aeternus, -a, -um	everlasting, eternal
aliēnus, -a, -um	belonging to another, strange, foreign; unfavorable
alternus, -a, -um	alternating, by turns
altus, -a, -um	high, lofty; deep; nourished
amplus, -a, -um	extensive, spacious; splendid, glorious
antīquus, -a, -um	ancient, old-time, former
anxius, -a, -um	anxious, troubled; troublesome, anxiety causing
aptus, -a, -um	fitted to, joined to; fit
asper, -era, -erum	rough; harsh, bitter
assiduus, -a, -um	constant, frequent

āter, ātra, ātrum	black, dark; gloomy, deadly
aureus, -a, -um	golden; splendid
avidus, -a, -um	craving, eager for, longing for, ardent
beātus, -a, -um	happy, prosperous, blessed, fortunate
benignus, -a, -um	kind, beneficit
blandus, -a, -um	alluring, charming
bonus, -a, -um	good
caecus, -a, -um	blind, unseeing; aimless; dark, obscure
caeruleus, -a, -um	dark blue, dark green, dark
candidus, -a, -um	white, fair
cārus, -a, -um	dear
castus, -a, -um	pure, spotless
cavus, -a, -um	hollow; enveloping
celsus, -a, -um	raised high, lofty
certus, -a, -um	fixed, settled, sure, certain
cēterus, -a, -um	the other; the remaining; in Pl used as *subst*: the others, the rest, all those remaining
citus, -a, -um	quick, rapid; early
clārus, -a, -um	bright; famous, distinguished
commodus, -a, -um	with due measure; suitable, convenient, comfortable
contentus, -a, -um	content, satisfied (+Ab); content with, pleased; se contentus: self contained; stretched, strained, exerted
crēber, -bra, -brum	thick, close, frequent, repeated, numerous
cultus, -a, -um	tilled, cultivated; tidy, neat; refined
cūnctus, -a, -um	all together, entire
cupidus, -a, -um	eager for, desirous of
dēnsus, -a, -um	thick, close, dense; murky; frequent
dexter, -t(e)ra, -t(e)rum	right , right hand
dīgnus, -a, -um	worthy
dīrus, -a, -um	dreadful

dīversus, -a, -um	turned away; different, diverse
dīvīnus, -a, -um	divine, godlike, inspired
dīvus, -a, -um	divine, blessed; saintly; *subst*: god, goddess
dubius, -a, -um	doubtful
dūrus, -a, -um	hard, tough, harsh
ēgregius, -a, -um	distinguished, uncommon
exiguus, -a, -um	limited, minute, scanty, little
exter extera -um	outward, external; outside, far; foreign, strange
extrēmus, -a, -um	outermost, farthest, last, extreme 50
falsus, -a, -um	deceptive, false
ferus, -a, -um	wild, fierce
fessus, -a, -um	faint, weary, tired
fēstus, -a, -um	festive, festal
foedus, -a, -um	foul
fōrmōsus, -a, -um	finely formed, beautiful, handsome
frīgidus, -a, -um	cold
futūrus, -a, -um	about to be, future
gallus -a -um	Gallic
geminus, -a, -um	twin; twofold, double, two
graecus	Greek
grātus, -a, -um	acceptable, agreeable, pleasant; grateful
honestus, -a, -um	honorable
horridus, -a, -um	bristling, rough; terrible, fearful
hūmānus, -a, -um	pertaining to man, human; cultured, refined
īgnōtus, -a, -um	unknown
immēnsus, -a, -um	unmeasured, boundless
impius, -a, -um	impious
improbus, -a, -um	not good, wicked, depraved, rascally
incertus, -a, -um	uncertain

īnferus, -a, -um	low; vile; beneath; *subst*: those below, the dead
ingrātus, -a, -um	not acceptable, disagreeable; unfeeling
integer, -gra, -grum	untouched; fresh; complete, whole, uninjured; Pl, fresh troops
īrātus, -a, -um	angry
iūcundus, -a, -um	pleasant, agreeable
iūstus, -a, -um	right, just, fair
laetus, -a, -um	glad, joyful (used fig. of animals, countries, &c.)
largus, -a, -um	copious, lavish, unstinted
latinus	Latin
lātus, -a, -um	broad, wide
lentus, -a,- um	slow, sluggish, pliant
līber, -era, -erum	free
longus, -a, -um	long, far; tall; *smtms*: tedious
maestus, -a, -um	sad; mournful, mourning; stern, grim; inauspicious, ill-omened
magnus, -a, -um	great
malus, -a, -um	evil
mātūrus, -a, -um	ripe, mature; early, speedy
maximus, -a, -um	greatest
medius, -a, -um	mid, middle, central
merus, -a, -um	pure, unmixed
meus, -a, -um	my
minimus, -a, -um	smallest, least
mīrus, -a, -um	wonderful, marvelous
miser, -era, -erum	wretched, miserable
mortuus, -a, -um	dead
multi	from multus; *subst*: the many, the crowd, the common herd
multus, -a, -um	much; (Pl) many
mundus, -a -um	clean, elegant; refined, pure

necessarius -a -um	necessary, essential; inevitable; vital, private body parts
niger, -gra, -grum	black, dark; unlucky 100
nimius, -a, -um	too much, excessive
nitidus, -a, -um	bright, shining
niveus, -a, -um	snow-like, snow-white
nōnnullus, -a, -um	some, several
nocturnus, -a, -um	occurring at night, nightly
noster, -tra, -trum	our
nōtus, -a, -um	famous, known; infamous, notorious
novus, -a, -um	new
nūdus, -a, -um	naked, bare
obvius, -a, -um	in the way; easy; hostile; exposed to
optimus, -a, -um	best
paratus -a -um	prepared, ready; equipped
parvus, -a, -um	small, little
patrius, -a, -um	paternal, ancestral
paucus, -a, -um	few (Pl: paucī, -ae, -a)
paulus, -a, -um	little, small
perpetuus, -a, -um	unbroken, perpetual (of things but more usu. of time)
perterritus, -a, -um	terrified
pius, -a, -um	dutiful, devoted; just, filial, pious, kind, &c.
placidus, -a, -um	quiet, gentle, calm, kindly
plēnus, -a, -um	full
plerusque -aque -umque	for the most part, generally
plūrimus, -a, -um	most
posterus, -a, -um	next, later, subsequent
praecipuus, -a, -um	particular, specific
prīmus, -a, -um	first
prīscus, -a, -um	old-time, ancient, primitive

proprius, -a, -um	one's own; particular, peculiar
proximus, -a, -um	nearest
pūblicus, -a, -um	public
pulcher -chra -chrum	beautiful
purpureus, -a, -um	purple, crimson, red; eye-catching, bright
pūrus, -a, -um	clean, pure
quantus, -a, -um	how great? as great
rapidus, -a, -um	rapid, swift
rārus, -a, -um	wide apart, loose, thin; close; rare, seldom
rēctus, -a, -um	direct, straight
rēgius, -a, -um	kingly, royal
reliquus -a -um	remaining, rest, rest of; surviving
rōmanus -a -um	Roman
rūsticus, -a, -um	of the country, rural
sacer, -cra, -crum	sacred, holy, set apart, consecrated
saevus, -a, -um	fierce, raging, wrathful
sānctus, -a, -um	sacred, inviolable
sānus, -a, -um	sound of health, sane
scelestus, -a, -um	wicked, infamous; accursed
secundus, -a, -um	next, second, secondary, subordinate, following
sēcūrus, -a, -um	free from care, tranquil ; careless, reckless
serēnus, -a, -um	clear, calm, fair (esp. of weather)
singulus -a -um	apiece; one each; individual
sinister, -tra, -trum	left
sollicitus, -a, -um	thoroughly moved, excited; troubled
summus -a -um	highest, greatest, top (of)
superbus, -a, -um	overbearing; arrogant
superus	above, high, great
suprēmus, -a, -um	highest, loftiest, topmost; last, final
suus, -a, -um	his, his own, their, their own

150

stultus, -a, -um	stupid, foolish
tacitus, -a, -um	silent
tantus, -a, -um	so great, so much
tardus, -a, -um	slow, sluggish, lingering
tener, -era, -erum	tender
tertius, -a, -um	third
tūtus, -a, -um	safe, protected
ultimus, -a, -um	farthest (of space, time, quality, &c.)
vacuus, -a, -um	empty
vagus, -a, -um	strolling about, roaming; vagrant; wavering, unsteady, undependable, uncertain
validus, -a, -um	strong
vānus, -a, -um	containing nothing, empty; false, deceitful
varius, -a, -um	diversified, changing, varied, various
vāstus, -a, -um	empty, void, waste, wild, &c.
vērus, -a, -um	true, actual
vivus, -a, -um	alive, living

Irregular, –ius Gen, 2-1-2 Adjectives

There are only nine of these adjectives. In all cases of the plural, they are regular. See page 169 for more information on these forms.

alius, -a, -ud	other, another
alter, -era, -erum	other of two, one of two, second
neuter, -tra, -trum	neither of two
nūllus, -a, -um	not any, no one, no
sōlus, -a, -um	only, alone
tōtus, -a, -um	whole, entire
ūllus, -a, -um	any, any one
ūnus, -a, -um	one
uter, utra, utrum	one of two; which of the two

3.1 ADJECTIVES:
THIRD DECLENSION ADJECTIVES OF ONE
TERMINATION [13 ADJECTIVES]

	Singular		Plural	
	M/F	Nt	M/F	Nt
Nm	--*	--*	-ēs	-ia
Ac	-em	--	-ēs	-ia
Gn	-is	-is	-ium	-ium
Dt	-ī	-ī	-ibus	-ibus
Ab	-ī	-ī	-ibus	-ibus

*One Nom S ending covers all genders and is generally unpredictable. Furthermore, these words usually have stem changes. Thus, the lexicon provides the Nom S, and then the Gen S, which reveals the stem (by removing the -is).

āles, -itis	winged, swift, quick
audāx, -ācis	bold, daring; reckless; presumptuous
dīligens, -entis	careful, diligent
dīs, dītis	rich
dīves, -itis	rich; well off
fēlīx, -īcis	lucky
ferox, -īcis	ferocious, fierce
īnfēlīx, -īcis	unlucky
ingēns, -gentis	vast, huge, enormous, &c.
libēns, -entis	willing, with pleasure
memor, -is	mindful (of +Gn); remembering; commemorative
pār, paris	equal
potēns, potentis	mighty, powerful, potent

3.2 ADJECTIVES:
THIRD DECLENSION ADJECTIVES OF TWO TERMINATIONS [33 ADJECTIVES]

	Singular		Plural	
	M/F	Nt	M/F	Nt
Nm	-is	-e	-ēs	-ia
Ac	-em	-e	-ēs, -īs*	-ia
Gn	-is	-is	-ium	-ium
Dt	-ī	-ī	-ibus	-ibus
Ab	-ī	-ī	-ibus	-ibus

*Either ending may be used for either M or F in the Acc S.

brevis, -e	short, shallow, brief
caelestis, -e	from heaven; *subst*: the gods
commūnis, -e	ordinary; sociable; related; neutral; shared
crūdēlis, -e	cruel, pitiless, ruthless
dulcis, -e	sweet
difficilis, -e	difficult
facilis, -e	doable; practicable, easy
fidēlis, -e	faithful, loyal
fortis, -e	brave, valiant
grandis, -e	large, ponderous
gravis, -e	heavy (oft. in social or figural sense)
immortālis, -e	immortal
inānis, -e	void, empty; vain; foolish, pointless
īnsīgnis, -e	marked, distinguished, conspicuous
lēnis, -e	soft, gentle, mild

levis, -e	light; slight; trivial, unimportant
mītis, -e	mild, gentle
mollis, -e	soft, yielding, gentle
mortālis, -e	mortal; anything that has to do with humanity
nōbilis, -e	distinguished, noble; knowable
omnis, -e	all, every; as a whole
pinguis, -e	fat; rich, fertile
potis, -e	able, powerful
quālis, -e	of what kind, what nature; how made, constituted
rudis, -e	unwrought, untilled, unformed, rough, raw, wild; uncultivated, awkward, clumsy
similis, -e	like, similar
sublīmis, -e	raised up, elevated, on high
tālis, -e	such, of such a sort
tenuis, -e	stretched; thin, slender
trīstis, -e	sad, solemn, serious
turpis, -e	ugly, unsightly; disgraceful, foul
ūtilis, -e	useful
viridis, -e	verdant, green

3.3 ADJECTIVES:
THIRD DECLENSION ADJECTIVES
OF THREE TERMINATIONS [2 ADJECTIVES]

	Singular			Plural		
	M	F	Nt	M	F	Nt
Nm	-er	-is	-re	-ēs	-ēs	-ia
Ac	-em	-em	-re	-ēs, -īs*	-ēs	-ia
Gn	-is	-is	-is	-ium	-ium	-ium
Dt	-ī	-ī	-ī	-ibus	-ibus	-ibus
Ab	-ī	-ī	-ī	-ibus	-ibus	-ibus

*Either ending may be used for either M or F in the Acc P.

ācer, ācris, ācre	sharp, bitter, piercing; keen, sagacious; severe vigorous
celer, -eris, -ere	swift

OTHER ADJECTIVES

Comparative, Irregular, Indeclinable, Numerical
[13 adjectives]

centum	one hundred (indecl.)
duo, duae, duo	two
māior, māius	greater
melior, -ius	better
minor, minus	smaller, less

necesse	necessary; unavoidable; inevitable
plūs, plūris	more; a comparative form of multus
prior, prius	earlier, preceding, former
propior -pius	nearer, closer; more recent
quot	how many, as many (indcl.)
superior, -ius	higher, upper; former, previous, preceding; superior, more distinguished, greater
tot	so many (indcl.)
trēs, trēs, tria	three

ADVERBS

Adverbs are indeclinable. Of the 1,325 most common words in Classical Latin, 117 (about 9%) are adverbs.

adhūc	up to this (present), thus far
aliquando	sometime; at any time; finally; before too late; at length
aliter	otherwise, differently
bene	well
bis	twice
certē	surely, certainly, beyond doubt; at least, at any rate
ceterum	moreover; but yet; still, besides; in other respects.
circā	around, round about; as adv., round about, near
crās	tomorrow; (poet.) in the future
cūr	why?
dēniquē	at length, finally; to sum up, in word
dextera	on the right; on the right-hand side
diū	long, for a long time
eo	therefore, for that reason

ergō	therefore; on account of
etiam	and already; also, even
facile	easily, readily; generally, often; willingly, heedlessly
ferē	almost
forīs	without, abroad
forsitan	perhaps, perchance
fortē	by chance; perhaps, perchance; as luck would have it
frūstrā	in vain
haud	not
heri	yesterday
hodiē	today
hīc	here
hinc	hence
hūc	hither
iam	at that time, at this time
ibī (ibi)	there
ideo	therefore, for that reason
illīc	there
inde	thence (both of time and space)
interdum	meanwhile
intereā	meanwhile; ...in the interim, however,...
interim	meanwhile; at the same time; however
ita	in this way, in such a way, just so, thus
iterum	again, for the second time
libenter	willingly, gladly
longē	distant, far off; by far; for a long while
magis	more
magnoperē	greatly
male	badly, ill, wrongly, wickedly; extremely

maximē	very greatly; especially
mēcum	with me
minimē	very least; no
minus	less
modo	only, merely; just now / recently; presently
mox	soon, presently
multo	much, a great deal, very; most; by far 50
multum	much, greatly, plenty, very, more
ne (-ne)	particle, notes a question
neque	nor, and not, not, neither
nōn	not; (+ dum) not yet; (+ iam) no longer; non modo...sed etiam: not only...but also
nōndum	not yet
nonne...?	surely...?
num	whether; in question, expecting a negative reply: surely not...?
numquam	never
nunc	now
ōlim	at that time; formerly; *smtms:* hereafter
paene	almost
pariter	equally
parum	too little (minus & minime are used in cf.)
paulo	by a bit; by only a small amount
posteā	afterwards
postrīdiā	on the following day
potius	rather, more, preferably
praintereā	besides, moreover
prīmō	at first
prīmum	at first, in the first place
prius	earlier, previously, before
procul	at a distance, afar, from a distance

prope	nearly, almost
prōtinus	at once, right away; var. spelling: prōtenus
qua	on which side; at which place; in what direction, where; by what way
quam	how?; as; with comparatives: than; with superlatives: as *x* as possible
quamvīs	however you like; although
quandō	when...?; at some time
quantum	so much as, how much, how far
quārē (quā rē)	from what cause? why; by which means, whereby
quasi	as if
quemadmodum	in what way, how; as, just as; to the extent that
quidem	certainly, at least
quippe	of course, obviously
quō	to where...? to what purpose?
quomodo	how, in what way; just as
quondam	formerly, once upon a time
quoque	also, too
quotiē(n)s	how often
rūrsus (rūrsum)	turned back; back; on the other hand, in return; again
saepe	often
satis	enough, sufficiently, quite
scīlicet	one may know; certainly, of course
semel	once, a single time
semper	always, ever
sīc	in such a manner, so
sīcut (sīcutī)	just as
simul	at once, together, at the same time
simulac, simulatque	as soon as
solum	only, just barely, alone

100

57

statim	at once, immediately
subitō	suddenly, unexpectedly
tam	so
tantum	so much, so far; hardly, only
ter	three times
tum	then; finally; already
tunc	then
ubī (ubi)	where; *smtms:* a conj.: as soon as
umquam (unquam)	ever, at any time
unde	from where, from which, from whom
undique	from all sides, on all sides
utrum	whether; introducing an indirect question; utrum...an: whether...or
vehementer	violently, loudly
vel	even; or even; or; vel...vel either/or, whether/or
velut (velutī)	even as, like as, just as
vērō	in truth, but
vix	hardly, barely; with difficulty; reluctantly

CONJUNCTIONS

Conjunctions are indeclinable. Of the 1,325 most common words in Classical Latin, there are 42 conjunctions.

alii...alii	some...others
an	whether; can it be that... you don't mean that... (introducing a question that expects a negative answer, a further question)
anteā	before, in front of
antequam	before, sooner than; until
at	but, but yet

autem	moreover, but, however (always postpositive)
cum	when; as soon as; as, since (with subj.); (of concession) although (with subj.)
deinde	thereupon, then; next in order, furthermore
dum	while (with indic.); until (with subj.); provided that, assuming (with subj.)
enim	for, verily, you see
etiamsi	even if; although
igitur	accordingly, consequently, therefore
nam	for, because (*more emphatically*: namque)
namque	in fact, as a matter of fact, on the other hand
nē	lest, that not; (with verbs of fear) lest
nec (neque)	and not, nor, neither
nēve (neu)	and not, nor; nēve ... nēve (neu ... neu): neither...nor
nisī (nisi)	not if; if not; (after a neg.) unless, except; *si* is sometimes added"
postquam	after
quamquam	however, although (with indic.)
quandō	when?; since, because; si quando: if ever
que (-que)	and
quia	because
quīcumque, quaecumque, quodcumque	whoever, whichever, whatever
quīn	why not; in fact
quod	because; that; the fact that, insofar as
quoniam	since, whereas
sed	but
seu	or if
sī	if
sīve (seu)	if (alternate condition); sīve ... sīve: whether... or
tamen	still, nevertheless, notwithstanding

tamquam	so as, just as
tandem	at last, finally; do tell, pray tell me
ut (utī)	how; like, as; (often with correlatives as ita, sic) so; (temporal) as soon as
ve (-ve)	or (enclitic and reg. appended to first word in a clause)
ac	to, toward, at
atque	furthermore, and in addition, and also, and; than (after comparatives)
aut	or
dōnec	until
et	and
itaque	and so, therefore (reg. at beginning of sentence)

INTERJECTIONS

Interjections are indeclinable. Of the 1,325 most common words in Classical Latin, there are 4 interjections.

ecce	lo! behold!
heu or ēheu or eheu	alas!
iō	in joy: Yes! Hurrah!; grief: No! Oh! Woe!; calling attention: Look! Note! Mark!
ō	oh! ah!

PRONOUNS

The following pronouns occur frequently enough that they should be learned as part of the regular vocabulary, even though many are part of a larger conjugation. For example, *mihi* is the Dt S of *egō*, but both *egō* and *mihi* occur frequently enough to be learned as separate vocabulary entries. There are 32 such pronouns.

aliquis, aliquid	some, any
egō	I
hic, haec, hoc	this; the latter
īdem, eadem, idem	the same; + atque or the rel. pron., as
ille, illa, illud	that one; the former
ipse, ipsa, ipsum	self, selves
is, ea, id	he, she, it; that one, the one mentioned
iste, ista, istud	that
mē	me (Ac); by/from/with/ in me (Ab)
mihi	to/for me (Dt)
nōbīs	to, for, by, from, with, in us (Dt or Ab)
nōs	we, us (Nm or Ac)
nostri	our
quī, quae, quod	who, which (rel. Pro)
quīdam, quaedam, quiddam	a certain one, someone
quis	who? what?
quisquam, quidquam/ quicquam	any one
quisque, quaeque, quidque	whoever it be, whatever, each one, every
quisquis, quidquid/quicquid	whoever, whichever, everybody

sē or sēsē	himself, herself, itself, themselves (Ac S,Pl)
sē or sēse	by/from/with/ in himself, herself, itself, themselves (Ab S,Pl)
sibi	to/ for oneself (Dt)
sui	of him/her/itself, oneself (Gn)
tē	you (AcS); by/from/with/ in you (AbS)
tēcum	with you (sg.)
tibi	to/ for you (sg.)
tū tui	you (sg.)
tuus, -a, -um	your (sg.)
uterque, utraque, utrumque	each (of two); both; each one; either
vester, -tra, -trum	your (Pl)
vōbīs	to, for, by, from, with, in you (Pl)
vōs vestrum	you (Pl)

PREPOSITIONS

Of the 1,325 most common Latin words, 25 are prepositions.

ā (ab) (+Ab)	by (agent); from (departure, cause, or time)
ad (+Ac)	to, up to; towards; for, with regard to; according to; until, on, by
ante (+Ac)	before (space or time)
apud (+Ac)	at, by, near; in the presence of, view of, writings of
circum (+Ac)	around, around about, near; as adv., around, near, in a circle
contrā (+Ac)	against, opposite; as adv., facing, eye to eye; across
cum (+Ab)	with
dē (+Ab)	down from, from; concerning; according to

ex (+Ab)	out of, from (location or origin); according to; by reason of; because of
in (+Ac/Ab)	Ac: into, in the midst of, according to, for; Ab: in, on, within (time); in accordance with
inter (+Ac)	between, among; during
intrā (+Ac)	within
ob (+Ac)	on account of; for the sake of; instead of
per (+Ac)	through (location, time); during; by means of; (adv. in composition with adverbs and adjectives) very
post (+Ac)	after; as adv., afterwards
praeter (+Ac)	besides, except, contrary to; beyond (rank), in front of; more than
prō (+Ab)	in front of; on behalf of; in proportion to
propter (+Ac)	on account of; because of; by means of; (adv., very rare) near
sine (+Ab)	without (esp. in neg. phrases instead of *cum*)
sub (+Ac/Ab)	Ac: up to, under, close to (motion), until, before (time); Ab: under, beneath
super (+Ac/Ab)	Ac: upon, above, on top of; Ab: over, upon, concerning, during (time); *smtms* as adv: moreover, moreso
suprā (+Ac)	above, beyond; as adv., more, above, before, formerly
trans (+ Ac)	across, beyond
ultrā (+Ac)	beyond; as adv., beyond, further, on the other side, more than, besides
ūsque (+Ac)	all the way, up to (name of location); as adv., continuously

CHAPTER 2
TOPICAL LISTS

In this chapter, terms are gathered into conceptual groups for students who wish to concentrate on learning vocabulary by focusing on specific themes such as animals, human feelings, speaking and writing, adjectives of praise, adjectives of blame, and so forth.

Terms indented under a word are closely related to that word. Occasionally, a term will appear in *italics* and be preceded with a *"d."* These signs indicate words that might be easily confused with the main terms within the topical category and should be *distinguished* from them.

1. THE DIVINE

dea, -ae	goddess
deus, -ī	god
dīvīnus, -a, -um	divine, godlike, inspired
dīvus, -a, -um	divine, blessed; saintly; *subst*: god, goddess
	d. dīves rich
nympha, -ae	nymph
caelestis, -e	from heaven; *subst*: the gods
fātum, -ī	fate (lit. that which is spoken)
fortūna, -ae	fortune
sors, sortis	lot; fate, destiny, oracle; success
religiō, -ōnis	scruples; supernatural constraint, taboo; obligation; sanction; worship; rite; sanctity
templum, -ī	temple, holy place; place marked off for augury
āra, -ae	altar
vātēs, -is	prophet, soothsayer, seer, bard
vōtum, -ī	vow, sacred promise; prayer; sacred offering; vote

2. TIME

tempus, -oris	time; temple (beside the forehead)
aetās, -ātis	age, time of life
aevum, -ī	lifetime, age, old age; eternity
saeculum, -ī	an era, generation; age, esp. century; time in general
annus, -ī	year
hiem(p)s, hiemis	winter

vēr, vēris	spring
mēnsis, -is	month
d. mēnsa, -ae table	
hōra, -ae	hour
diēs, -ēī	day
nox, noctis	night
nocturnus, -a, -um	occurring at night, nightly
somnus, -ī	sleep
somnium, -ī	dream
tenebrae, -ārum	darkness (Pl only)
umbra, -ae	shade, shadow
moror, -āri, -ātus sum	to delay
mora, -ae	delay, hindrance; pause

3. Nature

A. Sky

mundus, -ī	universe, the world; the earth; the inhabitants of the earth, mankind
d. mundus -a -um elegant, refined	
orbis, -is	circle; territory; sphere
polus, -ī	pole (extremity of an axis); sky, heavens
caelum, -ī	sky; heaven
caelestis, -e	from heaven; *subst:* the gods
caeruleus, -a, -um	dark blue, dark green, dark
astrum, -ī	heavenly body, star, planet; constellation; sky
sīdus, -eris	star; constellation; *smtms:* weather (when Pl)
sōl, sōlis	sun
stēlla, -ae	star
aethēr, -eris	pure upper air, ether, heaven, sky

aura, -ae	breeze, breath of air; gleam; vapor; *Pl* airs, heaven
ventus, -ī	wind
imber, -bris	rain-storm, shower
nūbēs, -is	cloud, storm cloud; crowd, throng
fulmen, -inis	lightning; thunderbolt
nix, nivis	snow
niveus, -a, -um	snow-like, snow-white

B. Fire

ignis, -is	fire
flamma, -ae	flame, fire
fax, facis	torch
incendium, -ī	conflagration; glow, heat
cinis, -eris	ashes, embers

C. Water

aqua, -ae	water
fōns, fontis	spring, fountain
amnis, -is	river, torrent
flūmen, -inis	stream, river
rīpa, -ae	bank (of a river)
lacus, -ūs	lake (*smtms*: takes -ubus in Dt and Ab Pl)
fretum, -ī	strait (of water)
mare, -is	sea
pelagus, -ī	sea (esp. the open sea)
pontus, -ī	the open sea, deep
aequor, -oris	surface of the sea; any level smooth surface; a plain; the sea
unda, -ae	wave, billow; sea
gurges, -itis	gulf, whirlpool; sea

sinus, -ūs	fold; bosom of a robe; gulf, bay
lītus, -oris	beach, shore
ōra, -ae	coast
nāvis, -is	ship
ratis, -is	raft; vessel
classis, -is	class, division; fleet
vēlum, -ī	a cloth, covering; esp. sail

D. EARTH

terra, -ae	land (as opp. to water, air)
tellūs, -ūris	Earth
humus, -ī	ground
saxum, -ī	stone; stone face, cliff
antrum	cave, cavern, grot
mōns, montis	mountain
collis, -is	hill
campus, -ī	plain, field
ager, agrī	cultivated land, field, country
agricola, -ae	farmer, field worker
arvum, -ī	field; plowed land
rūs, rūris	country; (Pl) lands, fields
rūsticus, -a, -um	of the country, rural
lapis, -idis	stone
ferrum, -ī	iron; iron tool; weapon, sword
aes, aeris	copper, bronze; anything made of bronze
aurum, -ī	gold; money
aureus, -a, -um	golden; splendid

E. PLANTS

silva, -ae	forest, grove
nemus, -oris	open wood, glade; grove, forest; pasture
lūcus, -ī	grove; sacred grove
arbor, -oris	tree
rāmus, -ī	branch, bough (of a tree)
laurus, -ūs	bay-tree, laurel; wreath of laurel
sertum, -ī	wreath of flowers, garland
sēmen, -inis	seed
flōs, -ōris	flower, blossom; bloom; prime of youth
rosa, -ae	rose
flōreō, -ēre, -uī, --	to bloom
herba, -ae	herb; grass, turf, plant; meadow
messis, -is	a mowing, reaping, or ingathering of the corn, &c.; harvest; the harvested crops; harvest-time

F. ANIMALS

āles, -itis	winged, swift, quick
anguis, -is	serpent, snake
avis, -is	bird
bōs, bovis	ox
canis, -is	dog
cornū, -ūs	horn; beak; bow; trumpet; mountain peak; anything shaped like a horn
eques, -itis	horseman, rider; (Pl) cavalry; equestrian order
equus, -ī	horse
grex, gregis	herd
cf. ēgregius	*distinguished: lit. "out from the herd"*
leō, -ōnis	lion
nātus, -ī	son; (of animals) a young one; (Pl) offspring; *smtms*: nāta, -ae, f., for daughter

pecus, -udis	cattle (general expression for the larger variety of domestic animals)
pecus, -oris	cattle; sheep
d. pecūnia -ae	money
taurus, -ī	bull

4. PEOPLE

A. GENERAL

domina, -ae	householder, mistress, lady
dominus, -ī	householder, master, lord
fēmina, -ae	woman
mulier, -eris	woman (esp. married woman)
uxor, -ōris	wife
vir, virī	man; husband; hero
virtūs, -ūtis	manliness, valor, courage; virtues
coniūnx, -iugis	consort, spouse, husband or wife
māter, -tris	mother
pater, -tris	father
patria, -ae	fatherland, country
parēns, -entis	parent (used for either father or mother)
prōlēs, -is	offspring, descendants
nātus, -ī	son; (of animals) a young one; (Pl) offspring; *smtms*: nāta, -ae, f., for daughter
fīlia, -ae	daughter
fīlius, -ī	son
frāter, -tris	brother
soror, -ōris	sister
puella, -ae	girl; maiden

puer, puerī	boy; slave; (Pl) children
nepōs, -ōtis	grandson; descendant; spendthrift, prodigal, playboy
senex, -is	an old man; *smtms:* old woman
senectūs, -ūtis	old age
senātus, -ūs	council of elders, senate
gēns, gentis	family, tribe, race
genus, -eris	birth, origin, lineage; offspring; tribe, people; sort, kind
gignō, -ere	to beget; bear, bring forth
pariō, -ere	to bring forth, give birth to; accomplish, effect
d. parō, -āre	*to prepare, get ready; acquire*
d. pareō, -ēre	*to obey (+ Dt)*
adulēscēns, -entis	a youth, young man; young woman, maiden
barbarus, -ī	foreigner, stranger (of all but Greeks, Romans)
comes, -itis	comrade, companion
socius, -ī	ally, confederate
homō, -inis	person, man
hospes, -itis	host; guest, visitor, stranger; soldier in billets
hūmānus, -a, -um	pertaining to man, human; cultured, refined
minister, -trī	attendant, servant; tool, agent
pauper, -eris	a poor person
populus, -ī	people; nation
prīnceps, -ipis	the first person on a list; the one who originates, first delivers, an opinion; the first, the most eminent, most distinguished
prīncipium, -ī	beginning
pudor, -ōris	shame, modesty, propriety; sense of honor
turba, -ae	confusion, tumult; crowd, throng
vīcīnus, -ī	neighbour
virgō, -inis	maiden, virgin, girl

vulgō, -āre	to spread among the multitude; to make general, common, or universal; to put forth to the world; make known to all by words; publish
vulgus, -ī	the common people

B. THE BODY

corpus, -oris	body
auris, -is	ear
d. aura, -ae	*breeze, breath of air; gleam; vapor; Pl airs, heaven*
d. aurum, -ī	*gold; money*
capillus, -ī	head of hair, hair
caput, -itis	head
collum, -ī	neck
coma, -ae	hair, tresses
cor, cordis	heart
crīnis, -is	hair; locke of hair; plume of a helmet; tail of a comet
dexter, -t(e)ra, -t(e)rum	right , right hand
digitus, -ī	finger
faciēs, -ēī	form, figure, appearance, face
figūra, -ae	form, shape
fōrma, -ae	form, figure; structure, appearance; beauty
fōrmōsus, -a, -um	finely formed, beautiful, handsome
frōns, frontis	forehead, brow; front of a place
gena, -ae	cheek, eye
imāgō, -inis	image, form, figure, &c.
lingua, -ae	tongue; language
manus, -ūs	hand; crowd, group; band, a force
membrum, -ī	member, limb, organ; male genitals; room; section
oculus, -ī	eye

os, ossis	bone; kernal (nut); heartwood; pit or stone (fruit)
ōsculum, -ī	kiss
pectus, -oris	breast, bosom, chest; heart, soul, courage
pēs, pedis	foot
sanguis, -inis	blood
sinister, -tra, -trum	left
speciēs, -ēī	aspect, appearance
tergum, -ī	back, rear
vestīgium, -ī	footstep, footprint, track, trace
vestis, -is	grament, clothes; blanket; robe
vultus, -ūs	expression; face

C. MIND: MENTAL & SENSORY ACTIVITIES

videō, -ēre, vīdī, vīsus	to see; (pass.) be seen, seem, appear
invideō, -ēre, -vīdī, -vīsus	to look on, envy
invidia, -ae	envy, jealousy, hatred
cernō, -ere, crēvī, crētus	to see, make out; sift, discern, distinguish; examine; decide; separate, sift (rare)
decernō -ere decrevī -cretus	to decide, determine, resolve; decree; judge; vote for
tueor, -ērī, tuitus (tūtus) sum	to look at, look over; protect
tūtus, -a, -um	safe, protected
spectō, -āre, -āvī, -ātus	to look, face, look at, consider
exspectō, -āre, -āvī, -ātus	to look out; watch, wait, expect
aspiciō, -ere, -spexī, -spectus	to look to/at, behold
cōnspiciō, -ere, -spexī, -ectus	to catch sight of, behold
respiciō, -ere, -exī, -ectus	to look back, regard; give heed to, consider
audiō, -īre, -īvī, -ītus	to hear, listen to
vigilō, -āre, -āvī, -ātus	to be awake, be on guard

sentiō, -īre, sēnsī, sēnsus	to perceive by senses; feel, hear, see; perceive
sēnsus, -ūs	feeling, emotion, sense
sententia, -ae	feeling, thinking, opinion, judgment, &c.
intellegō, -ere, -lēxī, lēctus	to pick out from between; understand, be aware
sciō, scīre, scīvī (sciī), scītus	to know; know how
nesciō, -īre, -īvī, -ītus	to not know, be ignorant
nōscō, -ere, nōvī, nōtus	to come to know; (Prf.) know
cognōscō, -ere, -gnōvī, -nitus	to become acquainted with; recognize understand, learn
cēnseō, -ēre, -suī, -sus	to assess, rate, estimate; propose, determine, decide, think
reor, rērī, ratus sum	to reckon, calculate; think
cōgitō, -āre, -āvī, -ātus	to reflect, consider, think, draw together
cōgitātiō, -ōnis	meditation, thinking
cōnsulō, -ere, -luī, -ltus	to plan, deliberate consult; take thought for
d. cōnsul, -is	consul
cōnsilium, -ī	plan, idea, advice; council, deliberative body; prudence, discretion
arbitror, -ārī, -ātus sum	to serve as referee; consider; think, hold, deem
exīstimō, -āre, -āvī, -ātus	to form an opinion of; think; suppose
putō, -āre, -āvī, -ātus	to arrange, set in order; reckon, think; trim, clean
cōnstituō, -ere, -uī, -ūtus	to put together, establish, set up, station; determine
mēns, mentis	mind (the rational faculty)
ratiō, -ōnis	a thinking, reckoning; method, way; reasoning; account, invoice; system or plan; consideration or reason
causa, -ae	cause, motive; origin; occasion, subject; lawsuit, trial
īgnōtus, -a, -um	unknown

discō, -ere, didicī, discitus	to learn
doceō, -ēre, docuī, doctus	to teach; inform
crēdō, -ere, -didī, -ditus	to believe, trust
fallō, -ere, fefellī, falsus	to deceive, violate, betray; escape notice; dēceptus often serves as PPP
falsus, -a, -um	deceptive, false
dubitō, -āre, -āvī, -ātus	to doubt; deliberate; hesitate
dubius, -a, -um	doubtful
statuō, -ere, -uī, -ūtus	to set up, station, fix; resolve, determine
memorō, -āre, -āvī, -ātus	to recall, recount, relate
meminī, -isse, --	to remember; pay heed; be sure; Prf in form, Pr in meaning
memor, -is	mindful (of +Gn); remembering; unforgetting, commemorative
memoria, -ae	memory, recollection; history; that within memory; tradition

D. FEELINGS

anima, -ae	breeze; air; breath, spirit; life, soul (esp. in Pl)
animus, -ī	feeling, spirit, soul
ārdeō, -ēre, ārsī, ārsus	to burn; glow; be inflamed with desire
avidus, -a, -um	craving, eager for, longing for, ardent
cupiō, -ere, -īvī, -ītus	to long for, crave, desire
ingenium, -ī	character; temperament; ability
clēmentia, -ae	gentleness, mildness
fidēs, -eī	trust, faith; pledge, reliability, protection
furor, -ōris	rage; fury
īra, -ae	anger, wrath
īrāscor, -ī, iratus sum	to get angry
mālō, mālle, māluī, --	to wish more; prefer
nōlō, nōlle, nōluī, --	to be unwilling

sinō, -ere, sīvī, situs	to let go, allow, permit, suffer; (lit.) lay
soleō, -ēre, solitus sum	to be accustomed (semi-dep)
spērō, -āre, -āvī, -ātus	to hope
spēs, -eī	hope
volō, -āre, -āvī, -ātus	to will, wish, be willing
volucris, -is	bird; as adj., volucer, -cris, -cre: flying, winged
voluntās, -ātis	wish, desire
voluptās, -ātis	pleasure, enjoyment

E. SPEAKING & WRITING

dīcō, -ere, dīxī, dictus	to say, state, speak
āiō, --, --, --	to affirm, maintain, say yes
appellō, -āre, -āvī, -ātus	to accost, call, call upon
clāmor, -ōris	outcry, shout
imperō, -āre, -āvī, -ātus	to command; control
imperātor, -ōris	commander, general
d. imperium, -ī	*empire, power, command*
inquam (inquio)	I say; usu. placed after the first word or words of a quotation.
iubeō, -ēre, iussī, iussus	to bid, order
iūrō, -āre, -āvī, -ātus	to take an oath, swear
loquor, -ī, locūtus sum	to speak, talk
moneō, -ēre, -uī, -itus	to warn, advise
narrō, -āre, -āvī, -ātus	to relate, recount, narrate
negō, -āre, -āvī, -ātus	to say no, deny, refuse
nūntius, -ī	messenger; message, news
ōrātiō, -ōnis	a pleading, speech, address
ōrātor, -ōris	pleader, orator, spokesman
precor, -ārī, -ātus sum	to pray, supplicate, invoke

prex, precis	request, prayer (most freq. found in the Pl)
queror, -ī, questus sum	to complain of, lament
respondeō, -ēre, -spondī, -spōnsus	to reply, make answer; pledge in return
revocō, -āre, -āvī, -ātus	to call back, recall (lit. & fig.)
rogō, -āre, -āvī, -ātus	to ask, beg, request
sermō, -ōnis	conversation, discussion; diction; talk; word
sileō, -ēre, -uī, --	to be/keep quiet, still, silent, &c.
sonō, -āre, -nuī, -nitus	to sound, resound
sonus, -ī	sound, noise
taceō, -ēre, -uī, -itus	to be silent
tacitus, -a, -um	silent
tumultus, -ūs	commotion, uprising
verbum, -ī	word
vocō, -āre, -āvī, -ātus	to call, name
vōx, vōcis	voice; utterance, word
scrībō, -ere, scrīpsī, scrīptus	to write
auctor, -ōris	originator, producer, founder
fābula, -ae	a fictitious narrative, tale, story; dramatic poem, play; fable
littera, -ae	letter (of the alphabet); (Pl) literature, epistle, letters
titulus, -ī	inscription, label, title; notice, bill, placard; honourable appellation, title; pretext
cantō, -āre, -āvī, -ātus	to sing; play on an instrument
canō, -ere, cecinī, cantus	to sing
cantus, -ūs	song, music
carmen, -inis	song
chorus, -ī	dance, choral dance; band, troop
lyra, -ae	lute, lyre; lyric poetry, song; constellation Lyra

poēta, -ae	poet
versus, -ūs	rank, tier; verse; a turning

F. MILITARY AND THE STATE

cīvis, -is	citizen, fellow citizen
cīvitās, -ātis	community, city; citizens; rights, citizenship
iūs, iūris	right, law
iūstus, -a, -um	right, just, fair
iniūria, -ae	injustice, wrong, affront
iūdex, -icis	judge, juror, arbiter
lēx, lēgis	law, statute, ordinance (made by Senate and People)
respublica	res + publicus -a -um: the republic; *lit*: matters public
senātus, -ūs	council of elders, senate
corōna, -ae	garland, chaplet, wreath
forum, -ī	market-place; Roman forum; place of public meeting
cōnsul, -is	consul
eques, -itis	horseman, rider; Pl, cavalry; equestrian order
plebes, -ei	common people, general citizens; lower class; mob, the masses
vōtum, -ī	vow, sacred promise; prayer; sacred offering; vote
pūblicus, -a, -um	public, common, of the people
pareō, -ēre, parui, -titus	to obey (+ Dt)
d. pariō, -ere	*to bring forth, give birth to, bear; accomplish, effect*
d. parō, -āre	*to prepare, get ready; acquire*
mīles, -itis	soldier
d. mīlia, -ium (Pl)	*thousands; as adj., mīlle (indecl.)*
cohors, -tis	cohort, band; troop; yard, pen; crew of a ship; attendants, staff

legiō, -ōnis	legion
armō, -āre, -āvī, -ātus	to arm, equip
arma, -orum	(Pl) arms, armor; implements of war; gear, tackle
tēlum, -ī	weapon; bolt, javelin
arcus, -ūs	bow; arch
gladius, -ī	sword (prose); ēnsis, -is is the poet.
arx, arcis	citadel, castle; summit
moenia, -ium (Pl)	walls, fortifications
castra, -ōrum	camp (Pl only)
bellum, -ī	war
proelium, -ī	fight, battle
impetus, -ūs	charge, attack, rush
pāx, pācis	peace
sīgnum, -ī	sign, signal; mark, a seal; military standard
victor, -ōris	conqueror
victōria, -ae	victory
vincō, -ere, vīcī, victus	to conquer, vanquish
triumphus, -ī	triumph
praeda, -ae	booty, prey
hostis, -is	enemy; stranger, foreigner
custōs, -ōdis	guard, watchman
perīculum, -ī	danger, peril
praesidium, -ī	protection; help; guard; garrison
auxilium, -ī	support, assistance; (Pl) auxiliary forces, reinforcements

G. HONOR & APPORVAL

honor, -ōris	honor, praise, glory
honestus, -a, -um	honorable
laudō, -āre, -āvī, -ātus	to praise

laus, -dis	praise
fās, --	divine right or law; + inf., permissible to
nefās	anything contrary to divine law; impiety, wickedness; sin, abomination
glōria, -ae	glory, fame
fāma, -ae	rumor, reputation; fame, glory
grātia, -ae	favor; influence; gratitude; the Graces
grātus, -a, -um	acceptable, agreeable, pleasant; grateful
ingrātus, -a, -um	not acceptable, disagreeable; unfeeling
mōs, mōris	manner, way, custom, habit
mūnus, -eris	task, function, service; gift, offering; bribe
decus, -oris	glory, honor; deeds; dignity, decorum, beauty
amor, -ōris	love
amō, -āre, -āvī, -ātus	to love
amīcitia, -ae	friendship
amīcus, -ī	friend
complector, -ī, complexus sum	to entwine with, embrace, surround
nūbō, -ere, nūpsī, nuptus	to marry; to veil for the marriage ceremony
cūra, -ae	care, worry concern
cūrō, -āre, -āvī, -ātus	to care for; provide for; care to
sēcūrus, -a, -um	free from care, tranquil ; careless, reckless
dīligō, -ere, -lēxī, -lēctus	to choose, pick out; love, cherish
dīligēns, -entis	careful, diligent
probō, -āre, -āvī, -ātus	to find good, approve; prove
plaudō, -ere, plausī, plausus	to beat; flatter, clap
faveō, -ēre, fāvī, fautus	to favor
mīror, -ārī, -ātus sum	to wonder at, marvel at

mīrus, -a, -um	wonderful, marvelous
celebrō, -āre, -āvī, -ātus	to frequent, throng, crowd; celebrate, extol
libet, -ēre, libuit, libitua	it pleases
libēns, -entis	willing, with pleasure
placeō, -ēre, -uī, -itus	to please
placidus, -a, -um	quiet, gentle, calm, kindly
iuvō, -āre, iūvī, iūtus	to help, aid, assist; please, delight
iuvenis, -is	youth, young man or woman; Gn Pl takes -um)
iuventa, -ae	period of youth, youth
fruor, fruī, frūctus sum	to enjoy
frūctus, -ūs	fruit; produce; benefit, enjoyment
d. frūx, frūgis	fruit of any kind
gaudeō, -ēre, gāvīsus sum	to rejoice (semi-dep)
gaudium, -ī	delight, joy, pleasure
rīdeō, -ēre, rīsī, rīsus	to laugh, laugh at
lūdō, -ere, lūsī, lūsus	to play; make sport of
salūs, -ūtis	health; prosperity; greeting; salvation, safety
valeō, -ēre, -uī, -itūrus	to be strong (physically); (fig.) excel, be able, have power, be worth
validus, -a, -um	strong
optō, -āre, -āvī, -ātus	to choose, select; wish, desire
cupīdō, -inis	desire, eagerness, craving (often personified)
cupidus, -a, -um	eager for, desirous of
cupiō, -ere, -īvī, -ītus	to long for, crave, desire
studium, -ī	eagerness, devotion; (Pl) pursuits
audeō, -ēre, ausus sum	to be eager; dare, venture (semi- dep)
audāx, -ācis	bold, daring; reckless; presumptuous
d. audiō, -īre	to hear, listen to
certō, -āre, -āvī, -ātus	to make certain, decide (by contest); fight, contend, compete

H. DEATH, DISHONOR, & GRIEF

mors	death
mortālis, -e	mortal; anything that has to do with humanity
mortuus, -a, -um	dead
morior, morī, mortuus sum	to die
rogus, -ī	funeral pyre
sepulcrum, -ī	place of burial, tomb, grave
fūnus, -eris	funeral; death, dead body, pyre
lētum, -ī	ruin; (poetry) death
monumentum, -ī	reminder; memorial, monument
mānēs, -ium (Pl)	deifiied souls of the dead; ghosts, shades; gods of the Lower Word
morbus, -ī	sickness, disease
tumulus, -ī	hillock, mound; swelling
clādēs, -is	destruction, slaughter
crīmen, -inis	verdict, decision; charge, accusation
culpa, -ae	guilt, fault, blame
errō, -āre, -āvī, -ātus	to go astray, wander; err
error, -ōris	wandering; error, mistake, deception
īnsidia, -ae	a plot; treachery; trap; (Pl) ambush, ambuscade
lacrima, -ae	a tear, crying
fleō, -ēre, -ēvī, -ētus	to weep
poena, -ae	penalty, punishment
scelus, -eris	wicked deed, crime, sin
venēnum, -ī	poison; drug
vulnus, -eris	wound
caveō, -ēre, cāvī, cautus	to be on one's guard, beware
timeō, -ēre, -uī, --	to fear, dread
timor, -ōris	fear, apprehension

terreō, -ēre, -uī, -itus	to terrify, frighten
terror, -ōris	fright, terror, panic
patior, -ī, passus sum	to permit, endure
doleō, -ēre, doluī, dolitūs	to feel pain; grieve
dolor, -ōris	pain, grief; sorrow; resentment
vereor, -ērī, veritus sum	to fear, stand in awe of
metuō, -ere, -uī, --	to fear, apprehend, dread
metus, -ūs	fear, apprehension, dread
horreō, -ēre, -uī, --	to bristle; bristle at, shudder at
horridus, -a, -um	bristling, rough; terrible, fearful
maereō, -ēre, -uī, --	to grieve, mourn
maestus, -a, -um	sad; mournful, mourning; stern, grim; inauspicious, ill-omened
pudeō, -ēre, -uī, -itus	to make ashamed, put to shame; *smtms:* pudet, -ere
pudor, -ōris	shame, modesty, propriety; sense of honor
contemnō, -ere, -tempsī, -ptus	to despise, scorn, disdain
spernō, -ere, sprēvī, sprētus	to reject, despise, scorn; sever, remove

I. CITY AND BUILDINGS

urbs, urbis	city
via, -ae	way, route, street
obvius, -a, -um	in the way; easy; hostile; exposed to
mūrus, -ī	wall
domus, -ūs	home, house
vīlla, -ae	country-seat
līmen, -inis	threshold, lintel; door, house; smtms: barrier at a race
thalamus, -ī	bed-chamber, couch, (esp.) bridal bed
torus, -ī	bed, couch; royal seat or throne
iter, itineris	journey, route, line of march

labor, -ōris	toil, exertion
d. labor, lābī	*to glide, slip, slide*
opus, -eris	work
negotium, -ī	pain, trouble, distress; work, business, activity, job
pretium, -ī	price
ops, opis	assistance, aid; (Pl) means, resources
ōtium, -ī	leisure
quiēscō, -ere, -ēvī, -ētus	to go to rest; keep quiet, esp. sleep
quies quietis	quiet, calm, rest, peace; sleep
cibus, -ī	food
famēs, -is	hunger, famine
mēnsa, -ae	table
d. mēnsis, -is	*month*
pōculum, -ī	drinking cup
vīnum, -ī	wine; vine

J. ABSTRACTIONS & UNCLASSIFIED

causa, -ae	cause, motive; origin; occasion, subject; lawsuit, trial
color, -ōris	color
cōpia, -ae	plenty, supply, abundance; (Pl) forces, esp. troops; supplies
exemplum, -ī	pattern; copy; analogy; archetype; reproduction, transcrption
fīnis, -is	end point, termination; boundary
locō, -āre, -āvī, -ātus	to place, locate; lend at interest
locus, -ī	place (Pl is Nt: -a, -a, -ōrum)
māteria, -ae	timber, lumber
modus, -ī	measure, manner, kind
mōlēs, -is	lage mass; heap, pile; boulder; jetty, dam, dike; a monster

nātūra, -ae	nature
nēmō (nūllīus, nēminī, nēminem, nūllō)	no one
nihil or nīl (indecl.)	nothing
nōmen, -inis	name; (lit.) means of knowing
numerō, -āre, -āvī, -ātus	to count, reckon, number; pay, count out pay; number as one's own, have
numerus, -ī	number, amount; rhythm
ōrdō, -inis	succession, order, class, rank, row, &c.
pars, partis	part
pondus, -eris	weight (both lit. and fig.)
rēs, reī	thing (used in innumerable senses and in very many phrases)
rota, -ae	wheel
spatium, -ī	space (of time, usually; *smtms*: of place)
vicis, vicis	turn, change, succession; exchange, repayment; plight, lot
vis, vīs (defective)	force, strength, energy; (sg. vis,vīs,vim,vī,vī; Pl virēs, virēs, virium viribus, viribus)
vīta, -ae	life

5. DESTRUCTIVE ACTIONS

caedēs, -is	a cutting off; slaughter; gore
cadō, -ere, cecidī, cāsūrus	to fall; *smtms*: be slain
occīdō, -ere, -cīdī, -cīsus	to cut down, kill
laedō, -ere, laesī, laesus	to injure by striking, hurt
noceō, -ēre, -uī, -itus	to harm
feriō, -īre, --, --	to hit, strike; kill, deliver the death blow; strike a deal
d. ferō, ferre, tulī, lātum	to bear , carry, endure; declare
pūgnō, -āre, -āvī, -ātus	to fight
corrumpō, -ere, -rūpī, -ruptus	to break up, ruin, spoil, &c.

frangō, -ere, frēgī, frāctus	to break, shatter
negligō, -ere, -lēxī, lēctus	to disregard, neglect; ignore; despise
perdō, -ere, -didī, -ditus	to destroy, loose; put through
damnō, -āre, -āvī, -ātus	to inflict loss; condemn
pugna, -ae	battle, fight

6. Constructive Actions

faciō, -ere, fēcī, factus	to do, make (in many senses and phrases)
afficiō, -ere, -fēcī, -fectus	to do to (a person); affect, visit with
cōnficiō, -ere, -fēcī, -fectus	to make together; accomplish, complete; do up, exhaust
dēficiō, -ere, -fēcī, -fectus	to make away from; fail, give out; revolt from
efficiō, -ere, -fēcī, -fectus	to bring about, effect, complete; render
interficiō, -ere, -fēcī, -fectus	to make away with, kill, put to death
fīō, fierī (fīerī), factus sum	to become (*smtms*: used as Pr Ps of facio)
facilis, -e	doable; practicable, easy
officium, -ī	service, duty; kindness
fingō, -ere, fīnxī, fictus	to shape; invent; think
condō, -ere, -didī, -ditus	to put together, form; build, found; compose; store up; conceal
creō, -āre, -āvī, -ātus	to bring forth, produce, create; elect
ūtor, ūtī, ūsus sum	to use, employ (with Ab)
ūsus, -ūs	use, advantage; experience; ūsus est: it is necessary (+Ab)
ūtilis, -e	useful
ōrnō, -āre, -āvī, -ātus	to fit out, equip; embellish, adorn
alō, -ere, aluī, alitus	to nourish, feed; strengthen, sustain
altus, -a, -um	high, lofty; deep; nourished
colō, -ere, coluī, cultus	to till, cultivate; dwell in; cultivate, cherish, worship

cultus, -ūs	cultivation, care, tending; training, education, refinement; reverence
dēfendō, -ere, -endī, -ēnsus	to thrust off, ward off, defend
serviō, -īre, -īvī, -ītus	to be a slave, serve
servō, -āre, -āvī, -ātus	to save; keep, guard, watch over, protect
servus, -ī	slave

7. SUBJECT MOTION

eō, īre, iī (īvī), itus	to go
abeō, -īre, -iī, -itus	to go away, depart
adeō, -īre, -iī, -itus	to go to, visit; consult; enter upon, undergo
obeō, -īre, -iī (-īvī), -itus	to go toward, go to meet, traverse; enter upon, undergo; die
pereō, -īre, -iī, -itus	to go through; perish, be lost; also used as Ps of perdo
praetereō, -īre, -iī, -itus	to go by, pass, pass over
redeō, -īre, -iī, -itus	to go back, return
subeō, -īre, -iī, -itus	to go under, go up to; occur to; undergo, endure; (poetry) approach
trānseō, -īre, -iī, -itus	to go across, cross
petō, -ere, -īvī (-iī), -ītus	to fall upon, attack; aim at; seek, demand, ask for
repeto, -ere, -īvī (-iī), -ītus	to seek back, demand, exact; revisit; call to mind, recollect; repeat
properō, -āre, -āvī, -ātus	to hasten, speed
currō, -ere, cucurrī, cursus	to run
occurrō, -ere, occucurrī, occursus	to run to meet; oppose, resist; come to mind, occur (+ Dt)
cursus, -ūs	running; speed, zeal; charge; march; revolving (wheel); an advance
d. currus, -ūs	chariot
fluō, -ere, flūxī, flūxus	to flow
flūmen, -inis	stream, river

flūctus, -ūs	wave, flood, surge; tumult, disorder
veniō, -īre, vēnī, ventus	to come
conveniō, -īre, -vēnī, -ventus	to come together, assemble; meet
ēveniō, -īre, -vēnī, -ventus	to come forth; happen
inveniō, -īre, -vēnī, -ventus	to come upon, find; (rarely) find out
perveniō, -īre, -vēnī, -ventus	to get through, arrive, reach
cēdō, -ere, cessī, cessus	to move, step; go away; yield, retreat
accēdō, -ēre, -cessī, -cessus	to go to, move to, approach; be added (as pass. of addo); increase, wax
concēdō, -ēre, -cessī, -cessus	to go with; retire, withdraw; yield, submit; *smtms*: forgive
discēdō, -ēre, -cessī, -cessus	to divide, separate; go away, depart
prōcēd, -ēre, -cessī, -cessus	to go forth, advance
ēvādō, -ere, -vāsī, -vāsum	evade, escape; avoid
vadum, -ī	a ford; shallows, a shoal
vagus, -a, -um	roaming, strolling about; vagrant; wavering, unsteady, undependable, uncertain
fugiō, -ere, fūgī, fugitūrus	to flee, escape
fuga, -ae	flight, a running away, a route
vītō, -āre, -āvī, -ātus	to avoid, shun
vitium, -ī	flaw, defect, fault, crime
lateō, -ēre, -uī, --	to lie hid, be hidden; (with Ac. of person in poetry) be hid from, unknown
iaceō, -ēre, -uī, -itus	to lie down; lie ill, in ruins; sleep
d. iaciō, -ere	*to throw*
cadō, -ere, cecidī, cāsūrus	to fall; smtms: be slain
accidō, -ere, -cidī, --	to fall to; happen, suffer, experience (usu. in a bad sense)
cāsus, -ūs	a falling, fall; chance, accident
lābor, lābī, lāpsus sum	to glide, slip, slide

d. labor, -ōris	toil, exertion
ruō, -ere, ruī, rutus	to overthrow, throw down; rush down, tumble down
ruīna, -ae	downfall, collapse
surgō, -ere, surrēxī, surrēctus	to raise; rise
orior, orīrī, ortus sum	to arise; spring from, begin
exorior, -orīrī, -ortus sum	to rise up, appear, spring forth
dēscendō, -ere, -scendī, -scēnsus	to climb down, descend
stō, stāre, stetī, status	to stand
cōnstō, -stāre, -stitī, -stātūrus	to stand with, agree, be consistent with; be complete, regular; cost; it is established, certain
īnstō, -stāre, -stitī, -stātūrus	to follow; persist; labor at; menace; be at hand
praestō, -stāre, -stitī, -stitus	to stand in front, excel; exhibit, furnish
sedeō, -ēre, sēdī, sessus	to sit; be fixed, settled; *smtms:* to fit, suit
sēdēs, -is	seat; abode, habitation; (Gn Pl -um)
maneō, -ēre, mānsī, mānsus	to remain, abide
occupō, -āre, -āvī, -ātus	to seize; overtake; capture, occupy; attack
intrō, -āre, -āvī, -ātus	to enter; penetrate
intrā (+Ac)	within
penetrō, -āre, -āvī, -ātus	to penetrate, react
tangō, -ere, tetigī, tāctus	to touch
contingō, -ere, -tigī, -tāctus	to touch, be contiguous to; happen to
haereō, haerēre, haesi, haesus	to stick, adhere, cling to; hesitate; be in difficulties
sequor, -ī, secūtus sum	to follow
cōnsequor, -ī, -secūtus sum	to follow up, overtake, attain
secundus, -a, -um	next, second, secondary, subordinate, following

8. SUBJECT STATUS

sum, esse, fuī, futūrus	to be, exist
absum, abesse, āfuī, āfutūrus	to be away, be absent
adsum (assum), adesse, adfuī (affuī), adfutūrus (affutūrus)	to be present, be at hand, assist
dēsum, deesse, dēfuī, defuturus	to be lacking, missing
prōsum, -desse, prōfuī, -futurus	to be profitable
supersum, -esse, -fuī, -futurus	to be over, remain, survive, &c.
futūrus, -a, -um	about to be, future
possum, posse, potuī	to be able, can
potēns, potentis	mighty, powerful, potent
potestās, -ātis	authority, just power
potis, -e	able, powerful
mereō, -ēre, -uī, -itus	to deserve, merit; serve (as a soldier)
nāscor, -ī, nātus sum	to be born (with many fig. uses)
nātus, -ī	son; (of animals) a young one; (Pl) offspring; *smtms:* nāta, -ae, for daughter
vīvō, -ere, vīxī, vīctūrus	to live, subsist
vivus, -a, -um	alive, living
spīrō, -āre, -āvī, -ātus	to breathe, blow
spīritus, -ūs	breathing, breath; breath of life, life; high spirit, pride, courage
augeō, -ēre, auxī, auctus	to increase; exalt
crēscō, -ere, crēvī, crētus	to grow, increase
pateō, -ēre, -uī, --	to lie open, extend, spread
vireō, -ēre, -uī, --	to be verdant, green; be lively, vigorous
viridis, -e	verdant, green
palleō, -ēre, -uī, --	to be/look ash-coloured, wan, pale

ārdeō, -ēre, ārsī, ārsus	to burn; glow; be inflamed with desire
rubeō, -ēre, -uī, --	to grow red, redden, blush, colour up
ūrō, -ere, ussī, ustus	to burn
fulgeō, -ēre, fulsī, --	to shine brightly, gleam, flash
fulmen, -inis	lightning; thunderbolt
lūx, lūcis	light (of day)
lūceō, -ēre, lūxī, --	to be light, gleam, shine
lūmen, -inis	a light
lūna, -ae	moon
niteō, -ēre, -uī, --	to shine, glitter, gleam
nitidus, -a, -um	bright, shining
careō, -ēre, -uī, -itūrus	to be without, want
egeō, -ēre, -uī, --	to be destitute, lack
parcō, -ere, parcuī, parsūs	to spare, be sparing of
vacō, -āre, -āvī, -ātus	to be empty, open, unoccupied; be idle, free from.
vacuus, -a, -um	empty
imitor, -ārī, -ātus sum	to imitate

9. OBJECT MOTION, CHANGE OF LOCATION

moveō, -ēre, mōvī, mōtus	to move (lit. & fig.)
ferō, ferre, tulī, lātum	to bear , carry, endure; declare
afferō, afferre, attulī, allātus	to bring to, carry to (usually fig. of reports, news); (of emotions) excite
afferō, afferre, attulī, allātus	to bear away, bear off, take away, remove, &c.

cōnferō, -ferre, -tulī, collātus	to bring together, collect; bring to, transport; shift, transfer, compare
dēferō, -ferre, -tulī, -lātus	to bear away, carry away; report
differō, differre, distulī, dīlātus	to bear apart, differ; postpone; spread apart
īnferō, īnferre, intulī, illātus	to bear in, upon, come against; (bellum -) attack in war
offerō, -āre, -āvī, -ātus	to offer; present; bestow
perferō, -ferre, -tulī, -lātus	to bear through, carry through; endure to the end; carry news, announce
praeferō, -ferre, -tulī, -lātus	to bear before; place before, prefer; hand to; show, reveal
referō, referre, rettulī, relātum	to bear back, bring back; report, refer, announce
vehō, -ere, vēxī, vectus	to carry; (Ps.) be carried, ride, go, sail
gerō, gerere, gessī, gestus	to bear, carry; carry on, accomplish, manage
tollō, -ere, sustulī, sublātus	to raise up, exalt; acknowledge; weigh anchor;
trahō, -ere, trāxī, tractus	to drag, draw, draw in
dētrahō, -ere, -trāxī, -tractus	to draw off, pull off, rob
dūco, -ere, dūxī, ductus	to lead; deem, consider, hold
dēdūco, -ere, -dūxī, -ductus	to lead away; (of ships) launch; lead, bring into
ēdūco, -ere, -dūxī, -ductus	to bring up, rear, educate, lead
dux, ducis	leader, guide, general
mittō, -ere, mīsī, missus	to send, let go
āmittō, -ere, -mīsī, -missus	to let go away, lose; send away, dismiss
committō, -ere, -mīsī -missus	to join together; entrust; perform, do, allow
dīmittō, -ere, -mīsī, -missus	to send apart/away, despatch, dismiss, let go
permittō, -ere, -mīsī, -missus	allow to go through; to cut loose; to give up, entrust, commit; let fly, cast hurl; to yield, allow, permit

prōmittō, -ere, -mīsī, -missus	to permit to grow; proffer; promise, agree; let go forth
mandō, -āre, -āvī, -ātus	to hand over, commission
pellō, -ere, pepulī, pulsus	to strike, beat, push, drive (lit. & fig.)
impellō, -ere, -pulī, -pulsus	to drive on, impel; excite, urge on
agō, -ere, ēgī, āctus	to drive, carry on, do, act; treat, discuss; (of time) spend
agitō, -āre, -āvī, -ātus	to drive (esp. of hunters), to hound; to brandish
agmen, -inis	line of march; army on the march
cōgō, -ere, coēgī, coāctus	to drive together; gather; force, compel
exigō, -ere, -egī, exactus	to drive out, expel; examine, weigh
peragō, -ere, -ēgī, -āctus	to drive through; finish; accomplish
urgeō, -ēre, ursī, --	to drive, impel, press hard, urge
iaciō, -ere, iēcī, iactus	to throw

d. iaceō, -ēre   to lie down; lie ill, in ruins; sleep

iactō, -āre, -āvī, -ātus	to throw often, fling, toss; bandy words, vaunt
adiciō, -ere, -iēcī, -iectus	to add to, construct near to, be near to
obiciō, -ere, obiecī, -iectus	to throw before; object, oppose; upbraid
trāiciō, -ere, -iēcī, -iectus	to throw across; pass over; pierce
dō, dāre, dedī, datus	to give, put (latter meaning rare except in compounds)
addō, -ere, -didī, -ditus	to give to, add; add
circumdō, -dare, -dedī, -datus	to put around
prōdō, -ere, -didī, -ditum	to give forth, publish, hand down; give over, betray
reddō, -ere, -didī, -ditus	to give back, return; render
trādō, -ere, -didī, -ditus	to give over, hand over; entrust, yield
dōnō, -āre, -āvī, -ātus	to give, present as a gift
dōnum, -ī	gift, present

praebeō, -ēre, -buī, -bitus	to afford, furnish; hold in front
tribuō, -ere, -uī, -ūtus	to assign, bestow, grant, &c.
pōnō, -ere, posuī, positus	to put down, put, place, establish, &c.
compōnō, -ere, -posuī, -positus	to put together; build, construct, arrange; adjust, quiet, appease; bury, lay away
impōnō, -ere, -posuī, -positus	to put upon; impose, levy upon; put in
prōpōnō, -ere, -posuī, -positus	to put forward, set forth, propose, present, &c.
iungō, -ere, iūnxī, iūnctus	to join
iugum, -ī	yoke; ridge, chain of hills; summit
coniūnx (coniux), -iugis	consort, spouse, husband or wife
uxor, -ōris	wife
nectō, -ere, nex(u)ī, nexus	to bind, unite
fīgō, -ere, fīxī, fīxus	to fix, fasten; set up, establish; transfix, shoot
misceō, -ēre, miscuī, mixtus	to mix, mingle
pendō, -ere, pependī, pēnsus	to weigh, hang, suspend; pay
pendeō, -ēre, pependī, --	to hang, be suspended, in suspense
edō, -ere (or ēsse), ēdī, ēsus	to eat
bibō, -ere, bibī, --	to drink
hauriō, -īre, hausī, haustus	to draw (any fluid); *fig:* to take
fundō, -ere, fūdī, fūsus	to pour; scatter, disperse, rout
effundō, -ere, -fūdī, -fūsus	to pour out, pour forth
capiō, -ere, cēpī, captus	to take, seize
accipiō, -ere, -cēpī, -ceptus	to take to, i.e. receive, accept; suffer; learn
excipiō, -ere, -cēpī, -ceptus	to take out, take up; to except, relieve
incipiō, -ere, -cēpī, -ceptus	to take on, begin
recipiō, -ere, -cēpī, -ceptus	to take back, receive esp. one's due; (loosely) receive
rapiō, -ere, rapuī, raptus	to tear, seize, snatch

ēripiō, -ere, -ripuī, -reptus	to snatch away; save, rescue
carpō, -ere, carpsī, carptus	to pluck
sūmō, -ere, sūmpsī, sūmptus	to take up, take
habeō, -ēre, -uī, -itus	to have, hold, possess, cherish, contain, occupy, deem
prohibeō, -ēre, -uī, -itus	to hold forward; keep away, restrain
teneō, -ēre, tenuī, tentus	to hold, keep; to grasp; comprehend
contineō, -ēre, -tinuī, -tentus	to hold together; contain; bound, limit, restrain, &c. in many senses
pertineō, -ēre, -tinuī, --	to extend through; lead to, pertain to, bear upon
retineō, -ēre, -tinuī, -tentus	to hold back, detain; maintain, keep
sustineō, -ēre, -tinuī, -tentus	to hold under, i.e. hold up, sustain
relinquō, -ere, -līquī, -lictus	to leave behind, abandon
reliquus -a -um	remaining, rest, rest of; surviving
linquō, -ere, līquī, lictus	to leave, quit, forsake; abandon, desist; bequeath
dēserō, -ere, -seruī, -sertus	to disjoin, leave off, give up, abandon
pandō, -ere, pandī, passus	to spread, spread out; expand
spargō, -ere, -rsī, -rsus	to scatter
sternō, -ere, strāvī, strātus	to strew, spread out, stretch out; overthrow; devastate
quatiō, -ere, --, quassus	to shake
vertō, -ere, -rtī, -rsus	to turn; (Ps.) revolve
adversus, -a, -um	turned towards; facing, opposed; unfavorable
convertō, -ere, vertī, -versus	to turn about, turn, change
dīversus, -a, -um	turned away; different, diverse
revertō, -ere, -i, --	to turn back; return; recur
versō, -āre, -āvī, -ātus	to turn often, keep turning, wind; (pass.) move, be busy; dwell; conduct one's self
vertex (or vortex), -icis	whirl; top of a whirl; summit, head, height

volvō, -ere, volvī, volūtus	to roll, twist; turn over, revolve
aperiō, -īre, -ruī, -rtus	to uncover, open
experior, -īrī, expertus sum	to try thoroughly, test, experience
reperiō, -īre, -pperī, repertus	to find out (after search)
claudō, -ere, clausī, clausus	to close, shut

10. OBJECT STATUS, CHANGE OF STATUS

mūtō, -āre, -āvī, -ātus	to change
flectō, -ere, flexī, flexus	to bend, turn
torqueō, -ēre, torsi, tortus	to turn, twist; hurl; torture; bend, distort; spin
tendō, -ere, tetendī, tentus	to stretch
intendō, -ere, -tendī, -tentus	to stretch out, strain; *smtms*: determine (+ inf.)
ostendō, -ere, -tendī -tensus	to stretch towards, hold out; expose to view, show
terō, -ere, trīvī, trītus	to rub
premō, -ere, pressī, pressum	to press, press hard, pursue, overwhelm, &c.
opprimō, -ere, -pressī, -pressus	to press against; crush, overwhelm; surprise
regō, -ere, rēxī, rēctus	to guide, direct; esp. rule
rēctus, -a, -um	direct, straight
rēx, rēgis	king
regiō, -ōnis	direction, line; boundary, limit; district, region
rēgius, -a, -um	kingly, royal
rēgnō, -āre, -āvī, -ātus	to reign
rēgnum, -ī	royal power; control; kingdom
vinciō, -īre, vinxī, vinctus	to bind
vinculum, -ī	bond, fetter, tie

cingō, -ere, cinxī, cinctus	to encircle, surround, gird
solvō, -ere, solvī, solūtus	to loosen, release; set sail; perform, pay, fulfill
tegō, -ere, tēxī, tēctus	to cover; conceal
tēctum, -ī	a covered place; roof; building, house
dīvidō, -ere, -vīsī, -vīsus	to divide, separate
pingō, -ere, pīnxī, pictus	to paint; embroider; ornament; decorate
temperō, -āre, -āvī, -ātus	to divide or combine duly; to regulate, adjust; to qualify, temer, restrain, abstain
exstinguō, -ere, -stinxī, -stinctus	to quench, extinguish; kill; destroy
torreō, -ēre, torruī, tostus	to parch, scorch; (of a stream) rush
exerceō, -ēre, -uī, -itus	to keep on; keep busy; to work at; oversee
exercitus, -ūs	training; army
parō, -āre, -āvī, -ātus	to prepare, get ready; acquire
d. pareō, -ēre	*to obey (+ Dt)*
d. pariō, -ere	*to bring forth, give birth to, bear; accomplish, effect*
comparō, -āre, -āvī, -ātus	to get ready, provide; compare

11. ADJECTIVES

A. SIZE

magnus, -a, -um	great
māior, māius	greater
magnitūdō, -īnis	greatness, size
maximus, -a, -um	greatest
magis	more

d. magister, -trī	*master, schoolmaster; foreman, chief; steersman, teacher*
largus, -a, -um	copious, lavish, unstinted
grandis, -e	large, ponderous
immēnsus, -a, -um	unmeasured, boundless
ingēns, -gentis	vast, huge, enormous, &c.
tantus, -a, -um	so great, so much
quantus, -a, -um	how great? as great
altus, -a, -um	high, lofty; deep; nourished
lātus, -a, -um	broad, wide
d. latus, -eris	*side, flank*
parvus, -a, -um	small, little
parum	too little (minus & minime are used in cf.)
minimus, -a, -um	smallest, least
minor, minus	smaller, less
exiguus, -a, -um	limited, minute, scanty, little
tenuis, -e	stretched; thin, slender
longus, -a, -um	long, far; tall; *smtms*: tedious
brevis, -e	short, shallow, brief
gravis, -e	heavy (oft. in social or figural sense)
levis, -e	light; slight; trivial, unimportant
d. levō, -āre	*to lift; remove; lessen, relieve; make light*
amplus, -a, -um	extensive, spacious; splendid, glorious

B. NUMBER

aequus, -a, -um	level, even, equal; fair, kindly
pār, paris	equal
pariter	equally
quot	how many, as many (indcl.)
omnis, -e	all, every; as a whole

cūnctus, -a, -um	all together, entire
tōtus, -a, -um	whole, entire; (irr. gen. alterīus, dat. alterī)
tot	so many (indcl.)
multus, -a, -um	much; (Pl) many
plūs, plūris	more; a comparative form of multus
plūrimus, -a, -um	most
multitūdō, -inis	crowd, multitude; number, amount, body, a force; rabble, mob
paucus, -a, -um	few (Pl: paucī, -ae, -a)
paulus, -a, -um	little, small
rārus, -a, -um	wide apart, loose, thin; close; rare, seldom
nūllus, -a, -um	not any, no one, no; (irr. gen. alterīus, dat. alterī)
ūllus, -a, -um	any, any one; (irr. gen. alterīus, dat. alterī)
ūnus, -a, -um	one; (irr. gen. alterīus, dat. alterī)
sōlus, -a, -um	only, alone; (irr. gen. alterīus, dat. alterī)
prīmus, -a, -um	first
prior, prius	earlier, preceding, former
duo, duae, duo	two
geminus, -a, -um	twin; twofold, double, two
trēs, trēs, tria	three
ter	three times
tertius, -a, -um	third
centum	one hundred (indecl.)
mīlia, -ium (Pl)	thousands; as adj., mīlle (indecl.)

d. mīles, -itis   soldier

C. Texture & Density

ācer, ācris, ācre	sharp, bitter, piercing; keen, sagacious; severe vigorous
aciēs, -ēī	edge; front or line of battle
mollis, -e	soft, yielding, gentle

lēnis, -e	soft, gentle, mild
lentus, -a,- um	slow, sluggish, pliant
mītis, -e	mild, gentle
tener, -era, -erum	tender
plēnus, -a, -um	full
impleō, -ēre, -ēvī, -ētus	to fill in, fill up
inānis, -e	void, empty; vain; foolish, pointless
vānus, -a, -um	containing nothing, empty; false, deceitful
cavus, -a, -um	hollow; enveloping
dēnsus, -a, -um	thick, close, dense; murky; frequent
crēber, -bra, -brum	thick, close, frequent, repeated, numerous

D. APPEARANCE

āter, ātra, ātrum	black, dark; gloomy, deadly
niger, -gra, -grum	black, dark; unlucky
candidus, -a, -um	white, fair
nūdus, -a, -um	naked, bare
pinguis, -e	fat; rich, fertile
pulcher -chra -chrum	beautiful
purpureus, -a, -um	purple, crimson, red; eye-catching, bright

E. POSITION

celsus, -a, -um	raised high, lofty
sublīmis, -e	raised up, elevated, on high
commūnis, -e	ordinary; sociable; related; neutral; shared
extrēmus, -a, -um	outermost, farthest, last, extreme
īnferus, -a, -um	low; vile; beneath; *subst*: those below, the dead
medius, -a, -um	mid, middle, central

pūblicus, -a, -um   public

proprius, -a, -um one's own; particular, peculiar

F. TIME

aeternus, -a, -um	everlasting, eternal
immortālis, -e	immortal
perpetuus, -a, -um	unbroken, perpetual (of things but more usu. of time)
assiduus, -a, -um	constant, frequent
vetus, -eris	antiquity; Pl, ancient times; traditional ways; forefathers; as adj: old, of long standing
vetustās, -ātis	age; old age; antiquity; long duration
antīquus, -a, -um	ancient, old-time, former
prīscus, -a, -um	old-time, ancient, primitive
mātūrus, -a, -um	ripe, mature; early, speedy
novus, -a, -um	new
celer, -eris, -ere	swift
rapidus, -a, -um	rapid, swift
tardus, -a, -um	slow, sluggish, lingering

G. FAVORABLE

bonus, -a, -um	good
bene	well
melior, -ius	better
optimus, -a, -um	best
pius, -a, -um	dutiful, devoted; just, filial, pious, kind, &c.
pietās, -ātis	sense of duty, devotion, esp. between parents and children

impius, -a, -um	impious
fortis, -e	brave, valiant
nōbilis, -e	distinguished, noble; knowable
līber, -era, -erum	free
lībertās, -ātis	freedom, liberty
d. libellus, -ī	*booklet*
d. liber -brī	*book, volume; inner bark of the tree*
sānus, -a, -um	sound of health, sane
nōtus, -a, -um	famous, known; infamous, notorious
notō, -āre, -āvī, notātus	to note, mark out, watch, notice
īgnōtus, -a, -um	unknown
clārus, -a, -um	bright; famous, distinguished
praecipuus, -a, -um	particular, specific
īnsīgnis, -e	marked, distinguished, conspicuous
dīgnus, -a, -um	worthy
dīgnitās, -ātis	worth, rank, reputation, esteem, &c.
vērus, -a, -um	true, actual
vērō	in truth, but
fēlīx, -īcis	lucky
īnfēlīx, -īcis	unlucky
beātus, -a, -um	happy, prosperous, blessed, fortunate
laetus, -a, -um	glad, joyful (used fig. of animals, countries, &c.)
serēnus, -a, -um	clear, calm, fair (esp. of weather)
contentus, -a, -um	content, satisfied (+Ab); content with, pleased; se contentus: self contained; stretched, strained, exerted
dīves, -itis	rich; well off
d. dīvus -a -um	*divine, blessed; saintly*
ditiae, -ārum	riches (Pl only)
dīs, dītis	rich
dulcis, -e	sweet

blandus, -a, -um	alluring, charming
cārus, -a, -um	dear
iūcundus, -a, -um	pleasant, agreeable
commodus, -a, -um	with due measure; suitable, convenient, comfortable
pūrus, -a, -um	clean, pure
merus, -a, -um	pure, unmixed
integer, -gra, -grum	untouched; fresh, complete
castus, -a, -um	pure, spotless
d. castra, -ōrum	*camp (Pl only)*
sacer, -cra, -crum	sacred, holy, set apart, consecrated
sānctus, -a, -um	sacred, inviolable
fēstus, -a, -um	festive, festal

II. UNFAVORABLE

malus, -a, -um	evil
foedus, -a, -um	foul
turpis, -e	ugly, unsightly; disgraceful, foul
improbus, -a, -um	not good, wicked, depraved, rascally
crūdēlis, -e	cruel, pitiless, ruthless
ferus, -a, -um	wild, fierce
d. ferē	*almost*
saevus, -a, -um	fierce, raging, wrathful
asper, -era, -erum	rough; harsh, bitter
dūrus, -a, -um	hard, tough, harsh
vāstus, -a, -um	empty, void, waste, wild, &c.
miser, -era, -erum	wretched, miserable
trīstis, -e	sad, solemn, serious
sollicitus, -a, -um	thoroughly moved, excited; troubled
anxius, -a, -um	anxious, troubled; troublesome, anxiety causing

aeger, -gra, -grum	sick (body or soul)
fessus, -a, -um	faint, weary, tired
caecus, -a, -um	blind, unseeing; aimless; dark, obscure
rudis, -e	unwrought, untilled, unformed, rough, raw, wild; uncultivated, awkward, clumsy
avidus, -a, -um	craving, eager for, longing for, ardent

Chapter 3

Frequencies

The terms are here listed from the most frequently used to the least frequently used. The accompanying number   represents a permilliage score (%*m*), indicating how often one is likely to encounter a form of this word within a thousand words of "typical" Latin prose and poetry. Thus, a term with a frequency count of, for example, 3.1, is likely to be seen about three times in one thousand words of Latin text. On the other hand, a term with a frequency count of 0.5 will probably be seen once every two thousand words of reading; a count of 0.3 means a word will be seen once in every three thousand words read, while a term with a frequency count of .05 is likely to be met only about once in about every 20,000 words of typical Latin.

Of course, there is no such thing as "typical" Latin, since each author's style and emphases will differ, and the variations between the use of a word in prose and poetry are often dramatic. But the numbers given here are a reasonably solid measure of how often students are likely to encounter this word within their readings, across a broad range of Latin authors and texts.

LATIN VOCABULARY

Term	%m
quī quae quod	30.60
que (-que)	30.34
et	25.49
sum, esse	23.16
in (+Ak/Ab)	14.82
hic, haec, hoc	10.22
nōn	9.38
nec (neque)	6.78
is, ea, id	6.58
ut (utī)	6.50
ille, illa, illud	6.43
cum	6.42
sui	6.28
quis	5.99
ad (+Ak)	5.88
omnis, -e	5.45
ā (ab) (+Ab)	4.79
ēveniō, -īre	4.73
sī	4.69
sed	4.28
ipse, ipsa, ipsum	4.26
possum, posse	3.88
dīcō, -ere	3.81
per (+Ak)	3.79
suus, -a, -um	3.78
rēs, reī	3.77
meus, -a, -um	3.75
atque	3.58
mihi	3.49
vigilō, -āre	3.47
aut	3.43
iam	3.41

Term	%m
tē	3.28
ē, ex (+Ab)	3.27
tuus, -a, -um	3.22
faciō, -ere	3.18
dō, dāre	2.94
mē	2.85
tibi	2.77
sē	2.67
noster, -tra, -trum	2.65
habeō, -ēre	2.60
dē (+Ab)	2.51
deus, -ī	2.45
tū tui	2.38
feriō, -īre	2.37
diēs, -ēī	2.29
magnus, -a, -um	2.29
multus, -a, -um	2.29
ac	2.24
etiam	2.22
alius, -a, -ud	2.21
prīmus, -a, -um	2.20
nē	2.17
neque	2.13
tamen	2.10
nunc	2.09
animus, -ī	2.07
ūnus, -a, -um	2.04
tempus, -oris	2.01
veniō, -īre	2.01
egeō, -ēre	1.92
nūllus, -a, -um	1.89
tantus, -a, -um	1.80
modus, -ī	1.79

Term	%m
homō, -inis	1.77
sīc	1.75
vireō, -ēre	1.72
amor, -ōris	1.70
manus, -ūs	1.68
locus, -ī	1.64
nam	1.64
vitium, -ī	1.64
enim	1.63
malus, -a, -um	1.60
carmen, -inis	1.56
longus, -a, -um	1.56
corpus, -oris	1.54
volō, velle	1.53
quisque, quaeque, quidque	1.52
terra, -ae	1.51
inter (+Ak)	1.49
pars, partis	1.48
domus, -ūs	1.46
caelum, -ī	1.45
bonus, -a, -um	1.44
at	1.42
tōtus, -a, -um	1.40
amō, -āre	1.37
mors, -tis	1.36
nox, noctis	1.35
īdem, eadem, idem	1.32
tum	1.32
quidem	1.30
agō, -ere	1.28
bellum, -ī	1.28
nihil or nīl (indecl.)	1.28
nōmen, -inis	1.28

FRENQUENCIES

annus, -ī	1.27	vīvō, -ere	1.04	sacer, -cra, -crum	0.91
sōlus, -a, -um	1.27	magis	1.03	vis, vīs (defective)	0.91
ante (+Ak)	1.25	puer, puerī	1.03	māior, māius	0.90
quoque	1.25	tam	1.03	ne (-ne)	0.90
sine (+Ab)	1.24	causa, -ae	1.02	nōbīs	0.89
sub (+Ak/Ab)	1.24	dūco, -ere	1.02	iste, ista, istud	0.88
urbs, urbis	1.23	rēx, rēgis	1.02	prō (+Ab)	0.88
ō	1.22	māter, -tris	1.01	vereor, -ērī	0.88
vinculum, -ī	1.22	genus, -eris	1.00	autem	0.87
bonum, -ī	1.21	opus, -eris	1.00	mittō, -ere	0.87
pater, -tris	1.20	petō, -ere	1.00	referō, referre	0.87
quod	1.20	maximus, -a, -um	0.99	sōl, sōlis	0.87
malum, -ī	1.19	puella, -ae	0.99	ve (-ve)	0.87
superus	1.18	doceō, -ēre	0.98	vester, -tra, -trum	0.87
dum	1.16	iubeō, -ēre	0.98	fortūna, -ae	0.86
aliquis, aliquid	1.15	modo	0.97	altus, -a, -um	0.85
capiō, -ere	1.14	ita	0.97	pectus, -oris	0.84
beneficium, -ī	1.14	mīles, -itis	0.97	populus, -ī	0.84
saepe	1.13	quantus, -a, -um	0.96	putō, -āre	0.84
sibi	1.13	alter, -era, -erum	0.95	audiō, -īre	0.83
vel	1.13	crēber, -bra, -brum	0.95	canō, -ere	0.83
hostis, -is	1.11	mēns, mentis	0.95	cēterus, -a, -um	0.83
semper	1.11	novus, -a, -um	0.95	dulcis, -e	0.83
teneō, -ēre	1.10	rōmanus -a -um	0.95	pēs, pedis	0.83
vīta, -ae	1.10	nātūra, -ae	0.94	plūs, plūris	0.83
cūra, -ae	1.09	summus -a -um	0.94	versō, -āre	0.83
ignis, -is	1.09	gravis, -e	0.92	fortis, -e	0.82
os, ossis	1.09	fātum, -ī	0.91	stō, stāre	0.82
arma, -orum (pl.)	1.07	nisī (nisi)	0.91	vīcīnus, -ī	0.82
eō, īre	1.07	orbis, -is	0.91	fīō, fierī	0.81
quaerō, -ere	1.07	pōnō, -ere	0.91	legō, -ere	0.81
moveō, -ēre	1.05	proximus, -a, -um	0.91	nātus, -ī	0.81
ubī (ubi)	1.05	quīdam, quaedam, quiddam	0.91	vōx, vōcis	0.81

accipiō, -ere	0.80	gerō, gerere	0.70	vōtum, -ī	0.63
mōs, mōris	0.80	labor, -ōris	0.70	dūrus, -a, -um	0.62
sequor, sequī	0.80	simul	0.70	inquam, inquit	0.62
aqua, -ae	0.79	umbra, -ae	0.70	patria, -ae	0.62
ferus, -a, -um	0.79	honor, -ōris	0.69	solvō, -ere	0.61
loquor, -ī	0.79	iuvenis, -is	0.69	primum	0.60
mare, -is	0.79	unda, -ae	0.69	dīgnus, -a, -um	0.60
nōs	0.79	fidēs, -eī	0.68	eques, -itis	0.60
parēns, -entis	0.79	oculus, -ī	0.68	flamma, -ae	0.60
quis- quid- quicquam	0.79	relinquō, -ere	0.68	flūmen, -inis	0.60
post (+Ak)	0.78	scrībō, -ere	0.68	lūmen, -inis	0.60
amīcus, -ī	0.77	respublica	0.67	ventus, -ī	0.60
ars, artis	0.76	an	0.67	bene	0.59
lēx, lēgis	0.76	gēns, gentis	0.67	cēdō, -ere	0.59
ratiō, -ōnis	0.76	quisquis, quidquid	0.67	dominus, -ī	0.59
certus, -a, -um	0.75	vocō, -āre	0.67	duo, duae, duo	0.59
medius, -a, -um	0.75	dux, ducis	0.66	facilis, -e	0.59
quam	0.75	senex, -is	0.66	fēlīx, -īcis	0.59
ūllus, -a, -um	0.75	fleō, -ēre	0.65	iūs, iūris	0.59
dīvus, -a, -um	0.74	licet, -ēre	0.65	nōtus, -a, -um	0.59
levis, -e	0.74	orior, orīrī	0.65	ops, opis	0.59
miser, -era, -erum	0.74	parvus, -a, -um	0.65	rapiō, -ere	0.59
numquam	0.74	somnus, -ī	0.65	redeō, -īre	0.59
tantum	0.73	adsum, adesse	0.64	trīstis, -e	0.59
satis	0.73	cūnctus, -a, -um	0.64	vultus, -ūs	0.59
sīgnum, -ī	0.73	fīnis, -is	0.64	colō, -ere	0.58
aetās, -ātis	0.71	seu	0.64	condō, -ere	0.58
caput, -itis	0.71	aciēs, -ēī	0.63	deinde	0.58
fugiō, -ere	0.71	castra, -ōrum	0.63	flōs, -ōris	0.58
ingenium, -ī	0.71	cōnsilium, -ī	0.63	iaceō, -ēre	0.58
mūnus, -eris	0.71	equus, -ī	0.63	prōtinus	0.58
sciō, scīre	0.71	quīcumque	0.63	quia	0.58
vēr, vēris	0.71	sīdus, -eris	0.63	uterque	0.58

itaque	0.57	fāma, -ae	0.53	coniūnx, -iugis	0.48
lūx, lūcis	0.57	morior, morī	0.53	diū	0.48
mereō, -ēre	0.57	perīculum, -ī	0.53	metus, -ūs	0.48
mōns, montis	0.57	clārus, -a, -um	0.52	saevus, -a, -um	0.48
nōscō, -ere	0.57	parō, -āre	0.52	aeternus, -a, -um	0.47
reddō, -ere	0.57	timeō, -ēre	0.52	amnis, -is	0.47
silva, -ae	0.57	coma, -ae	0.51	cōgō, -ere	0.47
soleō, -ēre	0.57	cōnsul, -is	0.51	decus, -oris	0.47
turba, -ae	0.57	frāter, -tris	0.51	ergō	0.47
aurum, -ī	0.56	gallus -a -um	0.51	exercitus, -ūs	0.47
cadō, -ere	0.56	melior, -ius	0.51	extrēmus, -a, -um	0.47
hinc	0.56	nēmō	0.51	imperium, -ī	0.47
laus, -dis	0.56	nūmen, -inis	0.51	inde	0.47
proelium, -ī	0.56	tālis, -e	0.51	lātus, -a, -um	0.47
tener, -era, -erum	0.56	varius, -a, -um	0.51	mīror, -ārī	0.47
propior, -pius	0.55	viridis, -e	0.51	mundus, -a, -um	0.47
iter, itineris	0.55	sapiens sapientis	0.51	sentiō, -īre	0.47
lacrima, -ae	0.55	multum	0.51	tellūs, -ūris	0.47
numerus, -ī	0.55	legatus, -ī	0.50	aevum, -ī	0.46
pereō, -īre	0.55	cāsus, -ūs	0.50	anima, -ae	0.46
potis, -e	0.55	dēbeō, -ēre	0.50	dolor, -ōris	0.46
premō, -ere	0.55	minus	0.50	fōrma, -ae	0.46
rēgnum, -ī	0.55	sanguis, -inis	0.50	laetus, -a, -um	0.46
spēs, -eī	0.55	eo	0.50	līberī, -ōrum	0.46
tunc	0.55	adversus, -a, -um	0.49	mortālis, -e	0.46
vātēs, -is	0.55	audeō, -ēre	0.49	pār, paris	0.46
vivus, -a, -um	0.55	līber, -era, -erum	0.49	patior, -ī	0.46
coepī, -pisse, -ptus	0.54	marītus, -ī	0.49	paucus, -a, -um	0.46
studium, -ī	0.54	mīlia, -ium (pl.)	0.49	super (+Ac/Ab)	0.46
valeō, -ēre	0.54	pius, -a, -um	0.49	cōpia, -ae	0.45
vōs vestrum	0.54	placeō, -ēre	0.49	iuvō, -āre	0.45
adeō, -īre	0.53	quālis, -e	0.49	prīnceps, -ipis	0.45
apud (+Ak)	0.53	ager, agrī	0.48	assum adesse	0.45
campus, -ī	0.53				

Latin Vocabulary

aureus, -a, -um	0.44	quīn	0.42	cūr	0.38
cornū, -ūs	0.44	secundus, -a, -um	0.42	dea, -ae	0.38
lītus, -oris	0.44	ceterum	0.42	errō, -āre	0.38
mollis, -e	0.44	fūnus, -eris	0.41	fallō, -ere	0.38
plēnus, -a, -um	0.44	grātia, -ae	0.41	fōns, fontis	0.38
prōmittō, -ere	0.44	negō, -āre	0.41	hōra, -ae	0.38
quamvīs	0.44	pulcher -chra -chrum	0.41	iugum, -ī	0.38
umquam (unquam)	0.44	subeō, -īre	0.41	maneō, -ēre	0.38
ūsus, -ūs	0.44	vetustās, -ātis	0.41	membrum, -ī	0.38
vertex -icis	0.44	multi	0.41	misceō, -ēre	0.38
cernō, -ere	0.43	longe	0.41	mūtō, -āre	0.38
cognōscō, -ere	0.43	animal -malis	0.40	nāscor, -ī	0.38
cursus, -ūs	0.43	grātus, -a, -um	0.40	nōbilis, -e	0.38
dexter, -t(e)ra, -t(e)ri	0.43	hauriō, -īre	0.40	pateō, -ēre	0.38
gaudeō, -ēre	0.43	hymen, -is	0.40	poena, -ae	0.38
glōria, -ae	0.43	ingēns, -gentis	0.40	prōpōnō, -ere	0.38
hūc	0.43	ōrdō, -inis	0.40	saxum, -ī	0.38
hūmānus, -a, -um	0.43	parcō, -ere	0.40	sē	0.38
igitur	0.43	praestō, -stāre	0.40	similis, -e	0.38
īnferus, -a, -um	0.43	sēdēs, -is	0.40	sinus, -ūs	0.38
mūsa, -ae	0.43	vērus, -a, -um	0.40	sīve (seu)	0.38
postquam	0.43	cīvis, -is	0.39	tollō, -ere	0.38
procul	0.43	pāx, pācis	0.39	vehō, -ere	0.38
queror, -ī	0.43	regō, -ere	0.39	velut (velutī)	0.38
saeculum, -ī	0.43	reliquus -a -um	0.39	vestīgium, -ī	0.38
servō, -āre	0.43	unde	0.39	vulnus, -eris	0.38
sonō, -āre	0.43	occupō, -āre	0.38	provincia, -ae	0.38
templum, -ī	0.43	astrum, -ī	0.38	aequor, -oris	0.37
tot	0.43	candidus, -a, -um	0.38	avis, -is	0.37
vix	0.43	cārus, -a, -um	0.38	cōnferō, cōnferre	0.37
dēserō, -ere	0.42	cīvitās, -ātis	0.38	īra, -ae	0.37
iungō, -ere	0.42	comes, -itis	0.38	mox	0.37
pontus, -ī	0.42	cōnstō, -stāre	0.38	niger, -gra, -grum	0.37
quasi	0.42				

pariō, -ere	0.37	tentō, -āre	0.35	crēscō, -ere	0.33
sermō, -ōnis	0.37	plebes, -ei	0.35	frangō, -ere	0.33
speciēs, -ēī	0.37	quippe	0.34	fuga, -ae	0.33
tergum, -ī	0.37	exigō, -ere	0.34	līmen, -inis	0.33
trēs, trēs, tria	0.37	adhūc	0.34	minor, minus	0.33
tūtus, -a, -um	0.37	arbor, -oris	0.34	nesciō, -īre	0.33
ūtor, ūtī	0.37	auris, -is	0.34	poēta, -ae	0.33
abeō, -īre	0.36	beātus, -a, -um	0.34	propter (+Ak)	0.33
absum, abesse	0.36	brevis, -e	0.34	rīdeō, -ēre	0.33
cinis, -eris	0.36	caedēs, -is	0.34	torus, -ī	0.33
foedus, -a, -um	0.36	cantus, -ūs	0.34	odium, -ī	0.33
ibī (ibi)	0.36	cupiō, -ere	0.34	potius	0.33
incipiō, -ere	0.36	edō, -ere (or ēsse)	0.34	ideo	0.32
littera, -ae	0.36	fingō, -ere	0.34	addō, -ere	0.32
metuō, -ere	0.36	forem, -es, -et	0.34	dēficiō, -ere	0.32
nemus, -oris	0.36	iūstus, -a, -um	0.34	futūrus, -a, -um	0.32
prope	0.36	mēcum	0.34	lingua, -ae	0.32
sānctus, -a, -um	0.36	occīdō, -ere	0.34	lūna, -ae	0.32
soror, -ōris	0.36	proprius, -a, -um	0.34	moneō, -ēre	0.32
surgō, -ere	0.36	quamquam	0.34	ōs, ōris	0.32
trahō, -ere	0.36	quondam	0.34	perdō, -ere	0.32
ceteri, ceterorum	0.36	quoniam	0.34	precor, -ārī	0.32
aequus, -a, -um	0.35	rīpa, -ae	0.34	ultimus, -a, -um	0.32
inveniō, -īre	0.35	rumpō, -ere	0.34	ūsque (+Ak)	0.32
laudō, -āre	0.35	socius, -ī	0.34	dubitō, -āre	0.32
pondus, -eris	0.35	tēctum, -ī	0.34	ācer, ācris, ācre	0.31
sepulcrum, -ī	0.35	trādō, -ere	0.34	agmen, -inis	0.31
servus, -ī	0.35	uxor, -ōris	0.34	cōnficiō, -ere	0.31
tamquam	0.35	victōria, -ae	0.34	dīves, -itis	0.31
tēlum, -ī	0.35	volucris, -is	0.34	dōnō, -āre	0.31
vagus, -a, -um	0.35	oppidum, -ī	0.34	ferrum, -ī	0.31
exstinguō, -ere	0.35	qua	0.34	meminī, -isse	0.31
facile	0.35	contineō, -ēre	0.33	optimus, -a, -um	0.31

paulus, -a, -um	0.31	spatium, -ī	0.30	commūnis, -e	0.28
perveniō, -īre	0.31	triumphus, -ī	0.30	cōnsulō, -ere	0.28
pugna, -ae	0.31	vetus, -eris	0.30	contrā (+Ak)	0.28
pūrus, -a, -um	0.31	vīnum, -ī	0.30	dēnique	0.28
rogō, -āre	0.31	exeo, exīre	0.30	discō, -ere	0.28
rūrsus (rūrsum)	0.31	aliēnus, -a, -um	0.29	dīversus, -a, -um	0.28
rūs, rūris	0.31	arvum, -ī	0.29	efficiō, -ere	0.28
scelus, -eris	0.31	aura, -ae	0.29	falsus, -a, -um	0.28
superbus, -a, -um	0.31	claudō, -ere	0.29	fēmina, -ae	0.28
etiamsi	0.31	creō, -āre	0.29	fessus, -a, -um	0.28
aes, aeris	0.30	domina, -ae	0.29	fluō, -ere	0.28
ārdeō, -ēre	0.30	excipiō, -ere	0.29	imāgō, -inis	0.28
auctor, -ōris	0.30	imber, -bris	0.29	noceō, -ēre	0.28
celer, -eris, -ere	0.30	maestus, -a, -um	0.29	pelagus, -ī	0.28
citus, -a, -um	0.30	mālō, mālle	0.29	plūrimus, -a, -um	0.28
contingō, -ere	0.30	nil	0.29	reperiō, -īre	0.28
cor, cordis	0.30	ostendō, -ere	0.29	rosa, -ae	0.28
cupīdō, -inis	0.30	ōtium, -ī	0.29	voluptās, -ātis	0.28
ēripiō, -ere	0.30	respiciō, -ere	0.29	supplicium, -ī	0.28
fax, facis	0.30	singulus -a -um	0.29	certe	0.28
forīs	0.30	spargō, -ere	0.29	nostri	0.28
fundō, -ere	0.30	sūmō, -ere	0.29	occurrō, -ere	0.27
humus, -ī	0.30	supersum. -esse	0.29	dextera	0.27
invideō, -ēre	0.30	tardus, -a, -um	0.29	accēdō, -ēre	0.27
legiō, -ōnis	0.30	tenebrae, -ārum	0.29	agitō, -āre	0.27
mundus, -ī	0.30	intersum, -esse	0.29	careō, -ēre	0.27
namque	0.30	iudicium, -ī	0.29	dēsum, deesse	0.27
nōlō, nōlle	0.30	fera, -ae	0.29	impōnō, -ere	0.27
optō, -āre	0.30	male peius pessime	0.29	officium, -ī	0.27
permittō, -ere	0.30	aliquando	0.28	placidus, -a, -um	0.27
probō, -āre	0.30	auferō, auferre	0.28	porta, -ae	0.27
pūgnō, -āre	0.30	augeō, -ēre	0.28	praebeō, -ēre	0.27
rārus, -a, -um	0.30	color, -ōris	0.28	prior, prius	0.27

retineō, -ēre	0.27	ōlim	0.26	nāvis, -is	0.25
salūs, -ūtis	0.27	pendō, -ere	0.26	prōdō, -ere	0.25
timor, -ōris	0.27	praecipiō, -cipere	0.26	spectō, -āre	0.25
turpis, -e	0.27	pudor, -ōris	0.26	spērō, -āre	0.25
victor, -ōris	0.27	quārē (quā rē)	0.26	sustineō, -ēre	0.25
quemadmodum	0.27	recipiō, -ere	0.26	verbum, -ī	0.25
sapientia, -ae	0.27	rēctus, -a, -um	0.26	decernō -ere	0.25
verum, -ī	0.26	sedeō, -ēre	0.26	factum, -ī	0.25
quomodo	0.26	senātus, -ūs	0.26	torqueō, -ēre	0.24
āles, -itis	0.26	sors, sortis	0.26	affectus, -ūs	0.24
antīquus, -a, -um	0.26	stēlla, -ae	0.26	libido libidinis	0.24
arx, arcis	0.26	superō, -āre	0.26	negotium, -ī	0.24
blandus, -a, -um	0.26	tēcum	0.26	proficiscor, -cisci	**0.24**
castus, -a, -um	0.26	temptō, -āre	0.26	amīcitia, -ae	0.24
circā	0.26	statim	0.26	āmittō, -ere	0.24
complector, -	0.26	tribunus, -ī	0.26	conveniō, -īre	0.24
compōnō, -ere	0.26	forte	0.25	dēnsus, -a, -um	0.24
contemnō, -ere	0.26	facinus -noris	0.25	discēdō, -ēre	0.24
cūrō, -āre	0.26	aethēr, -eris	0.25	exīstimō, -āre	0.24
custōs, -ōdis	0.26	aspiciō, -ere	0.25	indicō, -āre	0.24
dīvitiae, -ārum	0.26	certō, -āre	0.25	iō	0.24
dōnum, -ī	0.26	chorus, -ī	0.25	īrāscor, -ī	0.24
frūstrā	0.26	cohors, -tis	0.25	lūdō, -ere	0.24
gaudium, -ī	0.26	crās	0.25	multitūdō, -inis	0.24
gignō, -ere	0.26	dēdūco, -ere	0.25	nix, nivis	0.24
īgnōtus, -a, -um	0.26	dubius, -a, -um	0.25	pariter	0.24
illīc	0.26	exspectō, -āre	0.25	pietās, -ātis	0.24
īnstituō, -ere	0.26	faveō, -ēre	0.25	plerusque -aque -umque	0.24
lacus, -ūs	0.26	fīlius, -ī	0.25	potēns, potentis	0.24
linquō, -ere	0.26	frōns, frontis	0.25	quiēscō, -ere	0.24
memoria, -ae	0.26	heu or ēheu or eheu	0.25	revocō, -āre	0.24
moror, -āri	0.26	iūdex, -icis	0.25	sēcūrus, -a, -um	0.24
nimius, -a, -um	0.26	memorō, -āre	0.25	sublīmis, -e	0.24

tandem	0.24	tegō, -ere	0.23	forsitan	0.22
tangō, -ere	0.24	ūrō, -ere	0.23	fretum, -ī	0.22
trānseō, -īre	0.24	videō, -ēre	0.23	fulmen, -inis	0.22
vacuus, -a, -um	0.24	haereō, haerēre	0.23	geminus, -a, -um	0.22
volō, -āre	0.24	paratus -a, -um	0.23	graecus	0.22
utrum	0.24	patrius, -a, -um	0.23	iaciō, -ere	0.22
aliter	0.24	quantum	0.23	immēnsus, -a, -um	0.22
caedō, -ere	0.24	gradus, gradus	0.23	impellō, -ere	0.22
initium, -ī	0.24	omittō, -ere	0.23	īnsīgnis, -e	0.22
motus, motus	0.23	intrō, -āre	0.22	iterum	0.22
opera, -ae	0.23	antequam	0.22	iūcundus, -a, -um	0.22
tempestas -tātis	0.23	offerō, -āre	0.22	iūrō, -āre	0.22
afferō, afferre	0.23	paulo	0.22	lapis, -idis	0.22
aperiō, -īre	0.23	aeger, -gra, -grum	0.22	laurus, -ūs	0.22
cingō, -ere	0.23	amplus, -a, -um	0.22	māteria, -ae	0.22
cōnsequor, -ī	0.23	appellō, -āre	0.22	memor, -is	0.22
crīmen, -inis	0.23	āra, -ae	0.22	mōlēs, -is	0.22
decet, -ēre	0.23	audāx, -ācis	0.22	niteō, -ēre	0.22
dēfendō, -ere	0.23	caveō, -ēre	0.22	niveus, -a, -um	0.22
fore	0.23	cavus, -a, -um	0.22	nocturnus, -a, -um	0.22
hīc	0.23	centum	0.22	nūbēs, -is	0.22
hospes, -itis	0.23	circum (+Ak)	0.22	nūdus, -a, -um	0.22
iactō, -āre	0.23	clāmor, -ōris	0.22	obeō, -īre	0.22
impetus, -ūs	0.23	colligō, -ere	0.22	pecūnia, -ae	0.22
impius, -a, -um	0.23	committō, -ere	0.22	pecus, -udis	0.22
īnferō, īnferre	0.23	concēdō, -ēre	0.22	pingō, -ere, pīnxī, pictus	0.22
magnitūdō, -īnis	0.23	dēsinō, -ere	0.22	praemium, -ī	0.22
parum	0.23	dīligō, -ere	0.22	praetereā	0.22
prex, precis	0.23	dīs, dītis	0.22	pretium, -ī	0.22
quotiē(n)s	0.23	ecce	0.22	prōlēs, -is	0.22
ratis, -is	0.23	faciēs, -ēī	0.22	quatiō, -ere	0.22
sternō, -ere	0.23	fēstus, -a, -um	0.22	rapidus, -a, -um	0.22
suprā (+Ak)	0.23	flectō, -ere	0.22	repeto, -ere	0.22

rogus, -ī	0.22	currus, -ūs	0.21	celsus, -a, -um	0.20
rudis, -e	0.22	dīvidō, -er	0.21	cēnseō, -ēre	0.20
serviō, -īre	0.22	doleō, -ēre	0.21	cessō, -āre	0.20
terō, -ere	0.22	fās	0.21	classis, -is	0.20
tertius, -a, -um	0.22	ferē	0.21	cōnstituō, -ere	0.20
urgeō, -ēre	0.22	furor, -ōris	0.21	convertō, -ere	0.20
vītō, -āre	0.22	improbus, -a, -um	0.21	crēdō, -ere	0.20
poetntia, -ae	0.22	lābor, lābī	0.21	crūdēlis, -e	0.20
contentus, -a, -um	0.22	leō, -ōnis	0.21	cultus, -a, -um	0.20
exsilium, -ī	0.22	libellus, -ī	0.21	dētrahō, -ere	0.20
integer, -a, -um	0.22	magister, -trī	0.21	difficilis, -e	0.20
multo	0.22	minister, -trī	0.21	digitus, -ī	0.20
obiciō, -ere	0.22	mīrus, -a, -um	0.21	dīgnitās, -ātis	0.20
solum	0.22	nūbō, -ere	0.21	exemplum, -ī	0.20
appareō, -ēre	0.22	nūntius, -ī	0.21	experior, -īrī	0.20
praeceptum, -ī	0.22	nympha, -ae	0.21	flūctus, -ūs	0.20
aestimō, -āre	0.21	ōrnō, -āre	0.21	haud	0.20
fateor, fateri	0.21	ōrō, -āre	0.21	honestus, -a, -um	0.20
philosophia, -ae	0.21	paene	0.21	īnstō, -stāre	0.20
consistō, -ere	0.21	pandō, -ere	0.21	integer, -gra, -grum	0.20
quies quietis	0.21	praetereō, -īre	0.21	interficiō, -ere	0.20
auctoritas -tatis	0.21	semel	0.21	latus -teris	0.20
cupiditas -tatis	0.21	spīritus, -ūs	0.21	merus, -a, -um	0.20
deligo, -ere	0.21	tacitus, -a, -um	0.21	moenia, -ium (pl.)	0.20
necessarius -a -um	0.21	taurus, -ī	0.21	mora, -ae	0.20
citō, -āre	0.21	vadum, -ī	0.21	necesse, necessis	0.20
sacrum, -ī	0.21	versus, -ūs	0.21	nuntiō, -āre	0.20
accidō, -ere	0.21	vincō, -ere	0.21	ōsculum, -ī	0.20
agricola, -ae	0.21	virtūs, -ūtis	0.21	pecus, -oris	0.20
āiō, --	0.21	exter extera -um	0.21	pellō, -ere	0.20
armō, -āre	0.21	alō, -ere	0.20	posterus, -a, -um	0.20
bibō, -ere	0.21	assiduus, -a, -um	0.20	prius	0.20
caecus, -a, -um	0.21	auxilium, -ī	0.20	prōiciō, -ere	0.20

115

pūblicus, -a, -um	0.20	mūrus, -ī	0.19	cibus, -ī	0.18
pudeō, -ēre	0.20	numerō, -āre	0.19	clādēs, -is	0.18
purpureus, -a, -um	0.20	obvius, -a, -um	0.19	collis, -is	0.18
quo	0.20	polus, -ī	0.19	collum, -ī	0.18
spīrō, -āre	0.20	praeter (+Ak)	0.19	cupidus, -a, -um	0.18
taceō, -ēre	0.20	prīncipium, -ī	0.19	damnō, -āre	0.18
thalamus, -ī	0.20	prōcēdō, -ēre	0.19	dēferō, dēferre	0.18
trāiciō, -ere	0.20	quandō	0.19	dēscendō, -ere	0.18
vertō, -ere	0.20	rāmus, -ī	0.19	dīmittō, -ere	0.18
vulgus, -ī	0.20	rēgius, -a, -um	0.19	dīvīnus, -a, -um	0.18
aptus, -a, -um	0.19	respondeō, -ēre	0.19	effugiō, -ere	0.18
asper, -era, -erum	0.19	sēnsus, -ūs	0.19	fīgō, -ere	0.18
caelestis, -e	0.19	sententia, -ae	0.19	figūra, -ae	0.18
capillus, -ī	0.19	serēnus, -a, -um	0.19	frīgidus, -a, -um	0.18
comparō, -āre	0.19	sollicitus, -a, -um	0.19	frīgus, -oris	0.18
corrumpō, -ere	0.19	suprēmus, -a, -um	0.19	frūctus, -ūs	0.18
crīnis, -is	0.19	temperō, -āre	0.19	fulgeō, -ēre, fulsī, --	0.18
currō, -ere	0.19	tendō, -ere	0.19	gena, -ae	0.18
differō, differre	0.19	tenuis, -e	0.19	hiem(p)s, hiemis	0.18
dōnec	0.19	tueor, -ērī	0.19	horridus, -a, -um	0.18
egō	0.19	vacō, -āre	0.19	hortor, -ārī	0.18
extera, -ae	0.19	vānus, -a, -um	0.19	imitor, -ārī	0.18
fābula, -ae	0.19	vestis, -is	0.19	ingrātus, -a, -um	0.18
frūx, frūgis	0.19	alternus, -a, -um	0.18	ingredior, -ī	0.18
gladius, -ī	0.19	antrum , -ī	0.18	iniūria, -ae	0.18
grex, gregis	0.19	arcus, -ūs	0.18	insula, -ae	0.18
imperō, -āre	0.19	avidus, -a, -um	0.18	intellegō, -ere	0.18
impleō, -ēre	0.19	barbarus, -ī	0.18	intendō, -ere	0.18
inānis, -e	0.19	bis	0.18	intrā (+Ak)	0.18
incertus, -a, -um	0.19	bōs, bovis	0.18	iuventa, -ae	0.18
īnsidia, -ae	0.19	caeruleus, -a, -um	0.18	largus, -a, -um	0.18
lēnis, -e	0.19	cantō, -āre	0.18	liber -brī	0.18
mītis, -e	0.19	celebrō, -āre	0.18	lībertās, -ātis	0.18

lūcus, -ī	0.18	torreō, -ēre	0.18	grandis, -e	0.17
mandō, -āre	0.18	tribuō, -ere	0.18	herba, -ae	0.17
minimus, -a, -um	0.18	ultrā (+Ak)	0.18	immortālis, -e	0.17
morbus, -ī	0.18	undique	0.18	imperātor, -ōris	0.17
negligō, -ere	0.18	ūtilis, -e	0.18	incendium, -ī	0.17
nēve (neu)	0.18	vērō	0.18	interdum	0.17
nōndum	0.18	via, -ae	0.18	interim	0.17
notō, -āre	0.18	vicis, vicis	0.18	invidia, -ae	0.17
ob (+Ak)	0.18	vinciō, -īre	0.18	labōrō, -āre	0.17
ōrātiō, -ōnis	0.18	virgō, -inis	0.18	laedō, -ere	0.17
pendeō, -ēre	0.18	vōbīs	0.18	latinus	0.17
peragō, -ere	0.18	voluntās, -ātis	0.18	lētum, -ī	0.17
perferō, -ferre	0.18	adiciō, -ere	0.17	levō, -āre	0.17
perpetuus, -a, -um	0.18	anguis, -is	0.17	libēns, -entis	0.17
pinguis, -e	0.18	āter, ātra, ātrum	0.17	locō, -āre	0.17
poscō, -ere	0.18	canis, -is	0.17	lūceō, -ēre	0.17
praesidium, -ī	0.18	cōgitātiō, -ōnis	0.17	lyra, -ae	0.17
prīmō	0.18	cōnor, -ārī	0.17	maereō, -ēre	0.17
prohibeō, -ēre	0.18	cōnspiciō, -ere	0.17	mānēs, -ium (pl.)	0.17
properō, -āre	0.18	corōna, -ae	0.17	mātūrus, -a, -um	0.17
prōsum, prōdesses	0.18	culpa, -ae	0.17	mēnsa, -ae	0.17
regiō, -ōnis	0.18	cultus, -ūs	0.17	monumentum, -ī	0.17
reor, rērī	0.18	dīligēns, -entis	0.17	mortuus, -a, -um	0.17
revertō, -ere	0.18	dīrus, -a, -um	0.17	mulier, -eris	0.17
ruō, -ere	0.18	effundō, -ere	0.17	narrō, -āre	0.17
sīcut (sīcutī)	0.18	ēgridior, -ī	0.17	nefās	0.17
somnium, -ī	0.18	error, -ōris	0.17	nitidus, -a, -um	0.17
sonus, -ī	0.18	exerceō, -ēre	0.17	ōra, -ae	0.17
spernō, -ere	0.18	famēs, -is	0.17	pareō, -ēre	0.17
superior, -ius	0.18	ferox, -īcis	0.17	pauper, -eris	0.17
ter	0.18	filia, -ae	0.17	penetrō, -āre	0.17
terreō, -ēre	0.18	fōrmōsus, -a, -um	0.17	pertineō, -ēre	0.17
terror, -ōris	0.18	fruor, fruī, frūctus sum	0.17	pōculum, -ī	0.17

portus, -ūs	0.17	gurges, -itis	0.16	subitō	0.16
praecipuus, -a, -um	0.17	horreō, -ēre	0.16	titulus, -ī	0.16
prīscus, -a, -um	0.17	īnfēlīx, -īcis	0.16	tumultus, -ūs	0.16
rēgnō, -āre	0.17	intereā	0.16	validus, -a, -um	0.16
resistō, -ere	0.17	īrātus, -a, -um	0.16	vāstus, -a, -um	0.16
ruīna, -ae	0.17	lar, laris	0.16	venēnum, -ī	0.16
sēmen, -inis	0.17	lateō, -ēre	0.16	habitō, -āre	0.15
sertum, -ī	0.17	lentus, -a,- um	0.16	incendō, -ere	0.15
sileō, -ēre	0.17	libet, -ēre	0.16	inimīcus, ī	0.15
tumulus, -ī	0.17	mēnsis, -is	0.16	emō, -ere	0.14
vēlum, -ī	0.17	messis, -is	0.16	hortus, -ī	0.14
vīlla, -ae	0.17	nectō, -ere	0.16	liberō, -āre	0.14
vir, virī	0.17	nepōs, -ōtis	0.16	posteā	0.14
volvō, -ere	0.17	oportet, -tēre	0.16	stultus, -a, -um	0.14
vulgō, -āre	0.17	opprimō, -ere	0.16	captīvus, -ī	0.13
adulēscēns, -entis	0.16	ōrātor, -ōris	0.16	consūmō, -ere	0.13
afficiō, -ere	0.16	palleō, -ēre	0.16	epistula, -ae	0.13
anxius, -a, -um	0.16	plaudō, -ere	0.16	num	0.13
arbitror, -ārī	0.16	potestās, -ātis	0.16	portō, -āre	0.13
carpō, -ere	0.16	praeda, -ae	0.16	fidēlis, -e	0.12
circumdō, -dare	0.16	praeferō, -ferre,	0.16	libenter	0.12
clēmentia, -ae	0.16	quō	0.16	quando	0.12
cōgitō, -āre	0.16	quot	0.16	vendō, -ere	0.12
commodus, -a, -um	0.16	religiō, -ōnis	0.16	ascendō, -ere	0.11
ēdūco, -ere	0.16	rota, -ae	0.16	dēleō, -ēre	0.11
ēgregius, -a, -um	0.16	rubeō, -ēre	0.16	festīnō, -āre	0.11
ēvādō, -ere	0.16	rūsticus, -a, -um	0.16	lībertus, -ī	0.11
exiguus, -a, -um	0.16	sānus, -a, -um	0.16	rēgīna, -ae	0.11
exorior, -orīrī	0.16	scīlicet	0.16	adveniō, -ire	0.10
ferō, ferre	0.16	senectūs, -ūtis	0.16	anteā	0.10
ferox, -īcis	0.16	sinister, -tra, -trum	0.16	benignus, -a, -um	0.10
flōreō, -ēre	0.16	sinō, -ere	0.16	celō, -āre	0.10
forum, -ī	0.16	statuō, -ere	0.16	clamō, -āre	0.10

Frenquencies

dormiō, -īre	0.10	nōnnullus, -a, -um	0.07	lacrimō, -āre	0.05
persuādeō, -ēre	0.10	trans (+ Ac)	0.07	ambulo, -āre	0.04
nauta, -ae	0.09	vulnerō, -āre	0.07	mercātor, -oris	0.04
necō, -āre	0.09	aedificō, -āre	0.06	scelestus, -a, -um	0.03
pūniō, -īre	0.09	invītō, -āre	0.06	taberna, -ae	0.03
senātor, -tōris	0.09	oppugnō, -āre	0.06	heri	0.02
vehementer	0.09	perterritus, -a, -um	0.06	magnoperē	< 0.02
cēna, -ae	0.08	regredior, regredi	0.06	minimē	< 0.02
custōdiō, -īre	0.08	salūto, -āre	0.06	postrīdiā	< 0.02
nonne	0.08	ancilla, -ae	0.05	simulac, -ulatque	< 0.02
hodiē	0.07	appropinquō, -āre	0.05	maximē	< 0.02
nāvigō, -āre	0.07				

119

CHAPTER 4

INDEX

This chpater presents an alphabetical index of all the terms contained in the list. The columns may be interpreted as follows:

Column A is the term itself.

Column B names the part of speech.

Column C indicates the grammatical grouping where one can find the word. Thus, the declensions of nouns and conjugations of verbs are supplied here, as appropriate.

Column D shows the *topical* category in which the word appears on pages 64 through 104. Not every term appears in one of the topcial lists, and if the term is not found there, this column will be blank.

Column E gives the frequency of the term, as outlined in the previous chapter.

The abbreviations for the grammatical groups in column C should be largely self explanatory, but just to be clear:

Nouns will show declension and gender. Thus, a third declension neuter noun will display 3n. Second declension masculine nouns will show 2m, and so forth.

Verbs will simply show their conjugations; a "d" or "sd" shown as a suffix indicates a deponent or semideponent verb, respectively.

Adjectives will display 212 for those taking masculine, feminine and neuter endings from the II, I & II declension. Others will show 3 for III declension, followed by the number of terminations. Thus, III declension adjectives with two terminations will be seen as 3.2 while those with one termination will display 3.1.

Irregular and indeclinable terms will be given "irr" and "ind" respectively.

A	B	C	D	E
ā (ab) (+Ab)	prp	ind		4.79
abeō, -īre, -iī, -itus	v	irr	7	0.36
absum, abesse, āfuī, āfutūrus	v	irr	8	0.36
ac	cnj	ind		2.24
accēdō, -ēre, -cessī, -cessus	v	2	7	0.27
accidō, -ere, -cidī, --	v	3	7	0.21
accipiō, -ere, -cēpī, -ceptus	v	3-io	9	0.80
ācer, ācris, ācre	adj	3.3	11c	0.31
aciēs, -ēī	n	5f	11c	0.63
ad (+Ak)	prp	ind		5.88
addō, -ere, -didī, -ditus	v	3	9	0.32
adeō, -īre, -iī, -itus	v	irr	7	0.53
adhūc	adv	ind		0.34
adiciō, -ere, -iēcī, -iectus	v	3-io	9	0.17
adsum (assum), adesse, adfuī (affuī), adfutūrus (affutūrus)	v	irr	8	0.64
adulēscēns, -entis	n	3mf	4a	0.16
adveniō, -ire, -iī, -itus	v	4		0.10
adversus, -a, -um	adj	212	9	0.49
aedificō, -āre, -āvī, -ātus	v	1		0.06
aeger, -gra, -grum	adj	212	11h	0.22
aequor, -oris	n	3n	3c	0.37
aequus, -a, -um	adj	212	11b	0.35
aes, aeris	n	3n	3d	0.30
aestimō, -āre, -āvī, -ātus	v	1		0.21
aetās, -ātis	n	3f	2	0.71
aeternus, -a, -um	adj	212	11f	0.47
aethēr, -eris	n	3m	3a	0.25
aevum, -ī	n	2n	2	0.46
affectus, -ūs	n	4m		0.24

121

afferō, afferre, attulī, allātus	v	irr	9	0.23
afficiō, -ere, -fēcī, -fectus	v	3-io	6	0.16
ager, agrī	n	2m	3d	0.48
agitō, -āre, -āvī, -ātus	v	1	9	0.27
agmen, -inis	n	3n	9	0.31
agō, -ere, ēgī, āctus	v	3	9	1.28
agricola, -ae	n	1m	3d	0.21
āiō, --, --, --	v	irr	4e	0.21
āles, -itis	adj	3.1	3f	0.26
aliēnus, -a, -um	adj	212		0.29
aliquando	adv	ind		0.28
aliquis, aliquid	pro			1.15
aliter	adv	ind		0.24
alius, -a, -ud	adj	212-ius		2.21
alō, -ere, aluī, alitus	v	3	6	0.20
alter, -era, -erum	adj	212-ius		0.95
alternus, -a, -um	adj	212		0.18
altus, -a, -um	adj	212	11a	0.85
ambulo, -āre, -āvī, -ātus	v	1		0.04
amīcitia, -ae	n	1f	4g	0.24
amīcus, -ī	n	2m	4g	0.77
āmittō, -ere, -mīsī, -missus	v	3	9	0.24
amnis, -is	n	3m	3c	0.47
amō, -āre, -āvī, -ātus	v	1	4g	1.37
amor, -ōris	n	3m	4g	1.70
amplus, -a, -um	adj	212	11a	0.22
an	cnj	ind		0.67
ancilla, -ae	v	1f		0.05
anguis, -is	n	3mf	3f	0.17
anima, -ae	n	1f	4b	0.46
animal -malis	n	3n		0.40
animus, -ī	n	2m	4b	2.07

annus, -ī	n	2m	2	1.27
ante (+Ak)	prp	ind		1.25
anteā	cnj	ind		0.10
antequam	cnj	ind		0.22
antīquus, -a, -um	adj	212	11f	0.26
antrum , -ī	n	2n	3d	0.18
anxius, -a, -um	adj	212	11h	0.16
aperiō, -īre, -ruī, -rtus	v	4	9	0.23
appareō, -ēre, āruī, -itus	v	2		0.22
appellō, -āre, -āvī, -ātus	v	1	4e	0.22
appropinquō, -āre, -āvī, -ātus	v	1f		0.05
aptus, -a, -um	adj	212		0.19
apud (+Ak)	prp	ind		0.53
aqua, -ae	n	1f	3c	0.79
āra, -ae	n	1f	1	0.22
arbitror, -ārī, -ātus sum	v	1d	4c	0.16
arbor, -oris	n	3f	3e	0.34
arcus, -ūs	n	4m	4f	0.18
ārdeō, -ēre, ārsī, ārsus	v	2	8	0.30
arma, -orum (pl.)	n	2n	4f	1.07
armō, -āre, -āvī, -ātus	v	1	4f	0.21
ars, artis	n	3f	4e	0.76
arvum, -ī	n	2n	3d	0.29
arx, arcis	n	3f	4f	0.26
ascendō, -ere, ī, ascensus	v	3		0.11
asper, -era, -erum	adj	212	11h	0.19
aspiciō, -ere, -spexī, -spectus	v	3-io	4c	0.25
assiduus, -a, -um	adj	212	11f	0.20
assum adesse affui affuturus	v	irr		0.45
astrum, -ī	n	2n	3a	0.38
at	cnj	ind		1.42
āter, ātra, ātrum	adj	212	11d	0.17

123

atque	cnj	ind		3.58
auctor, -ōris	n	3mf	4e	0.30
auctoritas -tatis	n	3f		0.21
audāx, -ācis	adj	3.1	4g	0.22
audeō, -ēre, ausus sum	v	2sd	4g	0.49
audiō, -īre, -īvī, -ītus	v	4	4c	0.83
auferō, auferre, abstulī, ablātus	v	irr	9	0.28
augeō, -ēre, auxī, auctus	v	2	8	0.28
aura, -ae	n	1f	3a	0.29
aureus, -a, -um	adj	212	3d	0.44
auris, -is	n	3f	4c	0.34
aurum, -ī	n	2n	3d	0.56
aut	cnj	ind		3.43
autem	cnj	ind		0.87
auxilium, -ī	n	2n	4f	0.20
avidus, -a, -um	adj	212	11h	0.18
avis, -is	n	3f	3f	0.37
barbarus, -ī	n	2m	4a	0.18
beātus, -a, -um	adj	212	11g	0.34
bellum, -ī	n	2n	4f	1.28
bene	adv	ind	11g	0.59
beneficium, -ī	n	2n		1.14
benignus, -a, -um	adj	212		0.10
bibō, -ere, bibī, --	v	3	9	0.21
bis	adv	ind		0.18
blandus, -a, -um	adj	212	11g	0.26
bonum, -ī	n	2n		1.21
bonus, -a, -um	adj	212	11g	1.44
bōs, bovis	n	3mf	3f	0.18
brevis, -e	adj	3.2	11a	0.34
cadō, -ere, cecidī, cāsūrus	v	3	7	0.56
caecus, -a, -um	adj	212	11h	0.21

caedēs, -is	n	3f	5	0.34
caedō, -ere, caecidī, caesus	v	3		0.24
caelestis, -e	adj	3.2	3a	0.19
caelum, -ī	n	2n	3a	1.45
caeruleus, -a, -um	adj	212	3a	0.18
campus, -ī	n	2m	3d	0.53
candidus, -a, -um	adj	212	11d	0.38
canis, -is	n	3mf	3f	0.17
canō, -ere, cecinī, cantus	v	3	4e	0.83
cantō, -āre, -āvī, -ātus	v	1	4e	0.18
cantus, -ūs	n	4m	4e	0.34
capillus, -ī	n	2m	4b	0.19
capiō, -ere, cēpī, captus	v	3-io	9	1.14
captīvus, -ī	n	2m		0.13
caput, -itis	n	3n	4b	0.71
careō, -ēre, -uī, -itūrus	v	2	8	0.27
carmen, -inis	n	3n	4e	1.56
carpō, -ere, carpsī, carptus	v	3	9	0.16
cārus, -a, -um	adj	212	11g	0.38
castra, -ōrum	n	2n	4f	0.63
castus, -a, -um	adj	212	11g	0.26
cāsus, -ūs	n	4m	7	0.50
causa, -ae	n	1f	4j	1.02
caveō, -ēre, cāvī, cautus	v	2	4h	0.22
cavus, -a, -um	adj	212	11c	0.22
cēdō, -ere, cessī, cessus	v	3	7	0.59
celebrō, -āre, -āvī, -ātus	v	1	4g	0.18
celer, -eris, -ere	adj	3.3	11f	0.30
celō, -āre, -āvī, -ātus	v	1		0.10
celsus, -a, -um	adj	212	11e	0.20
cēna, -ae	n	1f		0.08
cēnseō, -ēre, -suī, -sus	v	2	4c	0.20

centum	adj	irr	11b	0.22
cernō, -ere, crēvī, crētus	v	3	4c	0.43
certe	adv	ind		0.28
certō, -āre, -āvī, -ātus	v	1	4g	0.25
certus, -a, -um	adj	212		0.75
cessō, -āre, -āvī, -ātus	v	1		0.20
ceteri, ceterorum	n	2n		0.36
ceterum	adv	ind		0.42
cēterus, -a, -um	adj	212		0.83
chorus, -ī	n	2m	4e	0.25
cibus, -ī	n	2m	4i	0.18
cingō, -ere, cinxī, cinctus	v	3	10	0.23
cinis, -eris	n	3m	3b	0.36
circā	adv	ind		0.26
circum (+Ak)	prp	ind		0.22
circumdō, -dare, -dedī, -datus	v	1	9	0.16
citō, -āre, -āvī, citātus	v	1		0.21
citus, -a, -um	adj	212	10	0.30
cīvis, -is	n	3mf	4f	0.39
cīvitās, -ātis	n	3f	4f	0.38
clādēs, -is	n	3f	4h	0.18
clamō, -āre, -āvī, -ātus	v	1		0.10
clāmor, -ōris	n	3m	4e	0.22
clārus, -a, -um	adj	212	11g	0.52
classis, -is	n	3f	3c	0.20
claudō, -ere, clausī, clausus	v	3	9	0.29
clēmentia, -ae	n	1f	4d	0.16
coepī, coepisse, coeptus	v	irr		0.54
cōgitātiō, -ōnis	n	3f	4c	0.17
cōgitō, -āre, -āvī, -ātus	v	1	4c	0.16
cognōscō, -ere, -gnōvī, -gnitus	v	3	4c	0.43
cōgō, -ere, coēgī, coāctus	v	3	9	0.47

cohors, -tis	n	3f	4f	0.25
colligō, -ere, -lēgī, -lēctus	v	3	4c	0.22
collis, -is	n	3m	3d	0.18
collum, -ī	n	2n	4b	0.18
colō, -ere, coluī, cultus	v	3	6	0.58
color, -ōris	n	3m	4j	0.28
coma, -ae	n	1f	4b	0.51
comes, -itis	n	3mf	4a	0.38
committō, -ere, -mīsī, -missus	v	3	9	0.22
commodus, -a, -um	adj	212	11g	0.16
commūnis, -e	adj	212	11e	0.28
comparō, -āre, -āvī, -ātus	v	1	10	0.19
complector, -ī, complexus sum	v	3d	4g	0.26
compōnō, -ere, -posuī, -positus	v	3	9	0.26
concēdō, -ēre, -cessī, -cessus	v	3	7	0.22
condō, -ere, -didī, -ditus	v	3	6	0.58
cōnferō, cōnferre, contulī, collātus	v	irr	9	0.37
cōnficiō, -ere, -fēcī, -fectus	v	3-io	6	0.31
coniūnx (coniux), -iugis	n	3mf	9	0.48
cōnor, -ārī, -ātus sum	v	1d		0.17
cōnsequor, -ī, -secūtus sum	v	3d	7	0.23
cōnsilium, -ī	n	2n	4e	0.63
consistō, -ere, constitī, constitus	v	3		0.21
cōnspiciō, -ere, -spexī, -spectus	v	3-io	4c	0.17
cōnstituō, -ere, -uī, -ūtus	v	3	4c	0.20
cōnstō, -stāre, -stitī, -stātūrus	v	1	7	0.38
cōnsul, -is	n	3m	4e	0.51
cōnsulō, -ere, -luī, -ltus	v	3	4e	0.28
cōnsūmō, -ere, -sūmpsī, -ūmptus	v	3		
contemnō, -ere, contempsī, -ptus	v	3	4h	0.26
contentus, -a, -um	adj	212	11g	0.22
contineō, -ēre, -tinuī, -tentus	v	2	9	0.33

contingō, -ere, -tigī, -tāctus	v	3	7	0.30
contrā (+Ak)	prp	ind		0.28
conveniō, -īre, -vēnī, -ventus	v	4	7	0.24
convertō, -ere, vertī, -versus	v	3	9	0.20
cōpia, -ae	n	1f	4j	0.45
cor, cordis	n	3n	4b	0.30
cornū, -ūs	n	4n	3f	0.44
corōna, -ae	n	1f	4f	0.17
corpus, -oris	n	3n	4b	1.54
corrumpō, -ere, -rūpī, -ruptus	v	3	5	0.19
crās	adv	ind		0.25
crēber, -bra, -brum	adj	212	11c	0.95
credo, -ere, -didī, -ditus	v	3	4c	0.20
creō, -āre, -āvī, -ātus	v	1	6	0.29
crēscō, -ere, crēvī, crētus	v	3	8	0.33
crīmen, -inis	n	3n	4h	0.23
crīnis, -is	n	3m	4b	0.19
crūdēlis, -e	adj	3.2	11h	0.20
culpa, -ae	n	1f	4h	0.17
cultus, -ūs	n	4m		0.17
cultus, -a, -um	adj	212	6	0.20
cum	cnj/ prep	ind		6.42
cūnctus, -a, -um	adj	212	11b	0.64
cupiditas -tatis	n	3f		0.21
cupīdō, -inis	n	3f	4g	0.30
cupidus, -a, -um	adj	212	4g	0.18
cupiō, -ere, -īvī, -ītus	v	3-io	4g	0.34
cūr	adv	ind		0.38
cūra, -ae	n	1f	4g	1.09
cūrō, -āre, -āvī, -ātus	v	1	4g	0.26
currō, -ere, cucurrī, cursus	v	3	7	0.19

currus, -ūs	n	4m	7	0.21
cursus, -ūs	n	4m	7	0.43
custōdiō, -īre, -īvī, -ītus	v	4		0.08
custōs, -ōdis	n	3mf	4f	0.26
damnō, -āre, -āvī, -ātus	v	1	5	0.18
dē (+Ab)	prp	ind		2.51
dea, -ae	n	1f	1	0.38
dēbeō, -ēre, -uī, -itus	v	2		0.50
decernō -ere decrevī decretus	v	3		0.25
decet, -ēre, decuit, --	v	2		0.23
decus, -oris	n	3n	4g	0.47
dēdūco, -ere, -dūxī, -ductus	v	3	9	0.25
dēfendō, -ere, -endī, -ēnsus	v	3	6	0.23
dēferō, dēferre, dētulī, dēlātus	v	irr	9	0.18
dēficiō, -ere, -fēcī, -fectus	v	3-io	6	0.32
deinde	cnj	ind		0.58
dēleō, -ēre, -evī, -etus	v	2		0.11
deligo, -ere, -ī, delectus	v	3		0.21
dēnique	adv	ind		0.28
dēnsus, -a, -um	adj	212	11c	0.24
dēscendō, -ere, -scendī, -scēnsus	v	3	7	0.18
dēserō, -ere, -seruī, -sertus	v	3	9	0.42
dēsinō, -ere, siī, situs	v	3	4c	0.22
dēsum, deesse, dēfuī, defuturus	v	irr	8	0.27
dētrahō, -ere, -trāxī, -tractus	v	3	9	0.20
deus, -ī	n	2m	1	2.45
dexter, -t(e)ra, -t(e)rum	adj	212	4b	0.43
dextera	adv	ind		0.27
dīcō, -ere, dīxī, dictus	v	3	4e	3.81
diēs, -ēī	n	5m	2	2.29
differō, differre, distulī, dīlātus	v	irr	9	0.19
difficilis, -e	adj	3.2		0.20

digitus, -ī	n	2m	4b	0.20
dīgnitās, -ātis	n	3f	11g	0.20
dīgnus, -a, -um	adj	212	11g	0.60
dīligēns, -entis	adj	3.1	4g	0.17
dīligō, -ere, -lēxī, -lēctus	v	3	4g	0.22
dīmittō, -ere, -mīsī, -missus	v	3	9	0.18
dīrus, -a, -um	adj	212		0.17
dīs, dītis	adj	3.1	11g	0.22
discēdō, -ere, -cessī, -cessus	v	3	7	0.24
discō, -ere, didicī, discitus	v	3	4c	0.28
diū	adv	ind		0.48
dīversus, -a, -um	adj	212	9	0.28
dīves, -itis	adj	3.1	11g	0.31
dīvidō, -ere, -vīsī, -vīsus	v	3	10	0.21
dīvīnus, -a, -um	adj	212	1	0.18
dīvitiae, -ārum	n	1f	11g	0.26
dīvus, -a, -um	adj	212	1	0.74
dō, dāre, dedī, datus	v	1	9	2.94
doceō, -ēre, docuī, doctus	v	2	4c	0.98
doleō, -ēre, doluī, dolitūs	v	2	4h	0.21
dolor, -ōris	n	3m	4h	0.46
domina, -ae	n	1f	4a	0.29
dominus, -ī	n	2m	4a	0.59
domus, -ūs	n	4f	4i	1.46
dōnec	cnj	ind		0.19
dōnō, -āre, -āvī, -ātus	v	1	9	0.31
dōnum, -ī	n	2n	9	0.26
dormiō, -īre, -īvī, -ītus	v	4		0.10
dubitō, -āre, -āvī, -ātus	v	1		0.32
dubius, -a, -um	adj	212	4c	0.25
dūco, -ere, dūxī, ductus	v	3	9	1.02
dulcis, -e	adj	3.2	11g	0.83

dum	cnj	ind		1.16
duo, duae, duo	adj	irr	11b	0.59
dūrus, -a, -um	adj	212	11h	0.62
dux, ducis	n	3m	9	0.66
ē, ex (+Ab)	prp	ind		3.27
ecce	intr	ind		0.22
edō, -ere (or ēsse), ēdī, ēsus	v	irr		0.34
ēdūco, -ere, -dūxī, -ductus	v	3	9	0.16
efficiō, -ere, -fēcī, -fectus	v	3-io	9	0.28
effugiō, -ere, -ūgī, -ūgitus	v	3-io		0.18
effundō, -ere, -fūdī, -fūsus	v	3	6	0.17
egeō, -ēre, -uī, --	v	2	9	1.92
egō	pro		8	0.19
ēgregius, -a, -um	adj	212		0.16
ēgridior, -ī, egressus sum	v	3d		0.17
emō, -ere, -emī, -emptus	v	3		0.14
enim	cnj	ind	3f	1.63
eo	adv	ind		0.50
eō, īre, iī (īvī), itus	v	irr		1.07
epistula, -ae	n	1f		0.13
eques, -itis	n	3m	7	0.60
equus, -ī	n	2m	3f	0.63
ergō	adv	ind	3f	0.47
ēripiō, -ere, -ripuī, -reptus	v	3-io		0.30
errō, -āre, -āvī, -ātus	v	1	9	0.38
error, -ōris	n	3m	4h	0.17
et	cnj	ind	4h	25.49
etiam	adv	ind		2.22
etiamsi	cnj	ind		0.31
ēvādō, -ere, -vāsî, -vāsum	v	3		0.16
ēveniō, -īre, -vēnī, -ventus	v	4	7	4.73
excipiō, -ere, -cēpī, -ceptus	v	3-io	9	0.29

131

exemplum, -ī	n	2n	4j	0.20
exeo, exīre, exivī, exitus	v	irr		0.30
exerceō, -ēre, -uī, -itus	v	2	10	0.17
exercitus, -ūs	n	4m	10	0.47
exigō, -ere, -egī, exactus	v	3		0.34
exiguus, -a, -um	adj	212	11a	0.16
exīstimō, -āre, -āvī, -ātus	v	1	4c	0.24
exorior, -orīrī, -ortus sum	v	4d	7	0.16
experior, -īrī, expertus sum	v	4d	9	0.20
exsilium, -ī	n	2n		0.22
exspectō, -āre, -āvī, -ātus	v	1	4c	0.25
exstinguō, -ere, -stinxī, -stinctus	v	3		0.35
exter extera -um	adj	212		0.21
extera, -ae	n	1f		0.19
extrēmus, -a, -um	adj	212	11e	0.47
fābula, -ae	n	1f	4e	0.19
faciēs, -ēī	n	5f	4b	0.22
facile	adv	ind		0.35
facilis, -e	adj	3.2	6	0.59
facinus -noris	n	3n		0.25
faciō, -ere, fēcī, factus	v	3-io	6	3.18
factum, -ī	n	2n		0.25
fallō, -ere, fefellī, falsus	v	3	4c	0.38
falsus, -a, -um	adj	212	4c	0.28
fāma, -ae	n	1f	4g	0.53
famēs, -is	n	3f	4i	0.17
fās	n	ind	4g	0.21
fateor, fateri, fassus sum	v	irr		0.21
fātum, -ī	n	2n	1	0.91
faveō, -ēre, fāvī, fautus	v	2	4g	0.25
fax, facis	n	3f	3b	0.30
fēlīx, -īcis	adj	3.1	11g	0.59

fēmina, -ae	n	1f	4a	0.28
fera, -ae	n	1f		0.29
ferē	adv	ind		0.21
feriō, -īre, --, --	v	4	5	2.37
ferō, ferre, tulī, lātum	v	irr	9	0.16
ferox, -īcis	adj	3.1		0.17
ferrum, -ī	n	2n	3d	0.31
ferus, -a, -um	adj	212	11h	0.79
fessus, -a, -um	adj	212	11h	0.28
festīnō, -āre, -āvī, -ātus	v	1		0.11
fēstus, -a, -um	adj	212	11g	0.22
fidēlis, -e	adj	3.2		0.12
fidēs, -eī	n	5f	4d	0.68
fīgō, -ere, fīxī, fīxus	v	3	9	0.18
figūra, -ae	n	1f	4b	0.18
fīlia, -ae	n	1f		0.12
fīlius, -ī	n	2m	4a	0.25
fingō, -ere, fīnxī, fictus	v	3	6	0.34
fīnis, -is	n	3m	4j	0.64
fīō, fierī (fīerī), factus sum	v	irr	6	0.81
flamma, -ae	n	1f	3b	0.60
flectō, -ere, flexī, flexus	v	3	10	0.22
fleō, -ēre, -ēvī, -ētus	v	2	4h	0.65
flōreō, -ēre, -uī, --	v	2	3e	0.16
flōs, -ōris	n	3m	3e	0.58
flūctus, -ūs	n	4m	7	0.20
flūmen, -inis	n	3n	7	0.60
fluō, -ere, flūxī, flūxus	v	3	7	0.28
foedus, -a, -um	adj	212	11h	0.36
fōns, fontis	n	3m	3c	0.38
fore	v	irr		0.23
forem, -es, -et	v	irr		0.34

forīs	adv	ind		0.30
fōrma, -ae	n	1f	4b	0.46
fōrmōsus, -a, -um	adj	212	4b	0.17
forsitan	adv	ind		0.22
forte	adv	ind		0.25
fortis, -e	adj	3.2	11g	0.82
fortūna, -ae	n	1f	1	0.86
forum, -ī	n	2n	4f	0.16
frangō, -ere, frēgī, frāctus	v	3	5	0.33
frāter, -tris	n	3m	4a	0.51
fretum, -ī	n	2n	3c	0.22
frīgidus, -a, -um	adj	212		0.18
frīgus, -oris	n	3n		0.18
frōns, frontis	n	3f	4b	0.25
frūctus, -ūs	n	4m	4g	0.18
fruor, fruī, frūctus sum	v	1d	4g	0.17
frūstrā	adv	ind		0.26
frūx, frūgis	n	3f	4g	0.19
fuga, -ae	n	1f	7	0.33
fugiō, -ere, fūgī, fugitūrus	v	3-io	7	0.71
fulgeō, -ēre, fulsī, --	v	2	8	0.18
fulmen, -inis	n	3n	8	0.22
fundō, -ere, fūdī, fūsus	v	3	9	0.30
fūnus, -eris	n	3n	4h	0.41
furor, -ōris	n	3m	4d	0.21
futūrus, -a, -um	adj	212	8	0.32
gallus -a -um	adj	212		0.51
gaudeō, -ēre, gāvīsus sum	v	2sd	4g	0.43
gaudium, -ī	n	2n	4g	0.26
geminus, -a, -um	adj	212	11b	0.22
gena, -ae	n	1f	4b	0.18
gēns, gentis	n	3f	4a	0.67

genus, -eris	n	3n	4a	1.00
gerō, gerere, gessī, gestus	v	3	9	0.70
gignō, -ere, genuī, genitus	v	3	4a	0.26
gladius, -ī	n	2m	4f	0.19
glōria, -ae	n	1f	4g	0.43
gradus, gradus	n	4m		0.23
graecus	adj	212		0.22
grandis, -e	adj	3.2	11a	0.17
grātia, -ae	n	1f	4g	0.41
grātus, -a, -um	adj	212	4g	0.40
gravis, -e	adj	3.2	11a	0.92
grex, gregis	n	3m	3f	0.19
gurges, -itis	n	3m	3c	0.16
habeō, -ēre, -uī, -itus	v	2	9	2.60
habitō, -āre, -āvī, -ātus	v	1		0.15
haereō, haerēre, haesi, haesus	v	2		0.23
haud	adv	ind		0.20
hauriō, -īre, hausī, haustus	v	4	9	0.40
herba, -ae	n	1f	3e	0.17
heri	adv	ind		0.02
heu or ēheu or eheu	intr	ind		0.25
hīc	adv	ind		0.23
hic, haec, hoc	pro			10.22
hiem(p)s, hiemis	n	3f	2	0.18
hinc	adv	ind		0.56
hodiē	adv	ind		0.07
homō, -inis	n	3m	4a	1.77
honestus, -a, -um	adj	212	4g	0.20
honor, -ōris	n	3m	4g	0.69
hōra, -ae	n	1f	2	0.38
horreō, -ēre, -uī, --	v	2	4h	0.16
horridus, -a, -um	adj	212	4h	0.18

hortor, -ārī, -ātus sum	v	1d		0.18
hortus, -ī	n	2d		0.14
hospes, -itis	n	3m	4a	0.23
hostis, -is	n	3mf	4f	1.11
hūc	adv	ind		0.43
hūmānus, -a, -um	adj	212	4a	0.43
humus, -ī	n	2f	3d	0.30
hymen, -is	n	3m		0.40
iaceō, -ēre, -uī, -itus	v	2	7	0.58
iaciō, -ere, iēcī, iactus	v	3-io	9	0.22
iactō, -āre, -āvī, -ātus	v	1	9	0.23
iam	adv	ind		3.41
ibī (ibi)	adv	ind		0.36
īdem, eadem, idem	pro			1.32
ideo	adv	ind		0.32
igitur	cnj	ind		0.43
ignis, -is	n	3m	3b	1.09
īgnōtus, -a, -um	adj	212	11g	0.26
ille, illa, illud	pro			6.43
illīc	adv	ind		0.26
imāgō, -inis	n	3f	4b	0.28
imber, -bris	n	3m	3a	0.29
imitor, -ārī, -ātus sum	v	1d	8	0.18
immēnsus, -a, -um	adj	212	11a	0.22
immortālis, -e	adj	3.2	11f	0.17
impellō, -ere, -pulī, -pulsus	v	3	9	0.22
imperātor, -ōris	n	3m	4e	0.17
imperium, -ī	n	2n	4e	0.47
imperō, -āre, -āvī, -ātus	v	1	4e	0.19
impetus, -ūs	n	4m	4f	0.23
impius, -a, -um	adj	212	11g	0.23
impleō, -ēre, -ēvī, -ētus	v	2	11c	0.19

impōnō, -ere, -posuī, -positus	v	3	9	0.27
improbus, -a, -um	adj	212	11h	0.21
in (+Ak/Ab)	prp	ind		14.82
inānis, -e	adj	3.2	11c	0.19
incendium, -ī	n	2n	3b	0.17
incendō, -ere, -dī, -incensus	v	3		0.15
incertus, -a, -um	adj	212		0.19
incipiō, -ere, -cēpī, -ceptus	v	3-io	9	0.36
inde	adv	ind		0.47
indicō, -āre, -āvī, -ātus	v	1	4e	0.24
īnfēlīx, -īcis	adj	3.1	11g	0.16
īnferō, īnferre, intulī, illātus	v	3	9	0.23
īnferus, -a, -um	adj	212	11e	0.43
ingenium, -ī	n	2n	4b	0.71
ingēns, -gentis	adj	3.1	11a	0.40
ingrātus, -a, -um	adj	212	4g	0.18
ingredior, -ī, ingressus sum	v	3d		0.18
inimīcus, ī	n	2m		0.15
initium, -ī	n	2n		0.24
iniūria, -ae	n	1f	4f	0.18
inquam, inquit, inquiunt, inquio, inquis	v	irr	4e	0.62
īnsidia, -ae	n	1f	4h	0.19
īnsīgnis, -e	adj	3.2	11g	0.22
īnstituō, -ere, -uī, -ūtus	v	3	4c	0.26
īnstō, -stāre, -stitī, -stātūrus	v	1	7	0.20
insula, -ae	n	1f		0.18
integer, -gra, -grum	adj	212	11g	0.22
intellegō, -ere, -lēxī, lēctus	v	3	4c	0.18
intendō, -ere, -tendī, -tentus	v	3	10	0.18
inter (+Ak)	prp	ind		1.49
interdum	adv	ind		0.17
intereā	adv	ind		0.16

interficiō, -ere, -fēcī, -fectus	v	3-io	6	0.20
interim	adv	ind		0.17
intersum, -esse, -fui, -futurus	v	irr		0.29
intrā (+Ak)	prp	ind	7	0.18
intrō, -āre, -āvī, -ātus	v	1		0.22
inveniō, -īre, -vēnī, -ventus	v	4	7	0.35
invideō, -ēre, -vīdī, -vīsus	v	2	4c	0.30
invidia, -ae	n	1f	4c	0.17
invītō, -āre, -āvī, -ātus	v	1		0.06
iō	intr	ind		0.24
ipse, ipsa, ipsum	pro			4.26
īra, -ae	n	1f	4d	0.37
īrāscor, -ī, iratus sum	v	3d	4d	0.24
īrātus, -a, -um	adj	212		0.16
is, ea, id	pro			6.58
iste, ista, istud	pro			0.88
ita	adv	ind		0.97
itaque	cnj	ind		0.57
iter, itineris	n	3n	4i	0.55
iterum	adv	ind		0.22
iubeō, -ēre, iussī, iussus	v	2	4e	0.98
iūcundus, -a, -um	adj	212	11g	0.22
iūdex, -icis	n	3m	4f	0.25
iudicium, -ī	n	2n		0.29
iugum, -ī	n	2n	9	0.38
iungō, -ere, iūnxī, iūnctus	v	3	9	0.42
iūrō, -āre, -āvī, -ātus	v	1	4e	0.22
iūs, iūris	n	3n	4f	0.59
iūstus, -a, -um	adj	212	4f	0.34
iuvenis, -is	n	3mf	4g	0.69
iuventa, -ae	n	1f	4g	0.18
iuvō, -āre, iūvī, iūtus	v	1	4g	0.45

labor, -ōris	n	3m	4i	0.70
lābor, lābī, lāpsus sum	v	3d	7	0.21
labōrō, -āre, -āvī, -ātus	v	1		0.17
lacrima, -ae	n	1f	4h	0.55
lacrimō, -āre, -āvī, -ātus	v	1		0.05
lacus, -ūs	n	4m	3c	0.26
laedō, -ere, laesī, laesus	v	3	5	0.17
laetus, -a, -um	adj	212	11g	0.46
lapis, -idis	n	3m	3d	0.22
lar, laris	n	3m		0.16
largus, -a, -um	adj	212	11a	0.18
lateō, -ēre, -uī, --	v	2	7	0.16
latinus	adj	212		0.17
latus -teris	n	3n		0.20
lātus, -a, -um	adj	212	11a	0.47
laudō, -āre, -āvī, -ātus	v	1	4g	0.35
laurus, -ūs	n	4f	3e	0.22
laus, -dis	n	3f	4g	0.56
legatus, -ī	n	2m		0.50
legiō, -ōnis	n	3f	4f	0.30
legō, -ere, lēgī, lēctus	v	3	4c	0.81
lēnis, -e	adj	3.2	11c	0.19
lentus, -a,- um	adj	212	11c	0.16
leō, -ōnis	n	3m	3f	0.21
lētum, -ī	n	2n	4h	0.17
levis, -e	adj	3.2	11a	0.74
levō, -āre, -āvī, -ātus	v	1	11a	0.17
lēx, lēgis	n	3f	4f	0.76
libellus, -ī	n	2m	11g	0.21
libēns, -entis	adj	3.1	4g	0.17
libenter	adv	ind		0.12
liber -brī	n	2m		0.18

līber, -era, -erum	adj	212	11g	0.49
līberī, -ōrum	n	2m		0.46
līberō, -āre, -āvī, -ātus	v	1		0.14
lībertās, -ātis	n	3f	11g	0.18
lībertus, -ī	n	2m		0.11
libet, -ēre, libuit, libitua	v	2	4g	0.16
libido libidinis	n	3f		0.24
licet, -ēre, -uit, licitus	v	2		0.65
līmen, -inis	n	3n	4i	0.33
lingua, -ae	n	1f	4b	0.32
linquō, -ere, līquī, lictus	v	3	9	0.26
littera, -ae	n	1f	4e	0.36
lītus, -oris	n	3n	3c	0.44
locō, -āre, -āvī, -ātus	v	1	4j	0.17
locus, -ī	n	2m	4j	1.64
longe	adv	ind		0.41
longus, -a, -um	adj	212	11a	1.56
loquor, -ī, locūtus sum	v	3d	4e	0.79
lūceō, -ēre, lūxī, --	v	2	8	0.17
lūcus, -ī	n	2m	3e	0.18
lūdō, -ere, lūsī, lūsus	v	3	4g	0.24
lūmen, -inis	n	3n	8	0.60
lūna, -ae	n	1f	8	0.32
lūx, lūcis	n	3f	8	0.57
lyra, -ae	n	1f	4e	0.17
maereō, -ēre, -uī, --	v	2	4h	0.17
maestus, -a, -um	adj	212	4h	0.29
magis	adv	ind	11a	1.03
magister, -trī	n	2m	11a	0.21
magnitūdō, -īnis	n	3f	11a	0.23
magnoperē	adv	ind		<0.02

magnus, -a, -um	adj	212	11a	2.29
māior, māius	adj	irr	11a	0.90
male peius pessime	adv	ind		0.29
mālō, mālle, māluī, --	v	irr	4c	0.29
malum, -ī	n	2n		1.19
malus, -a, -um	adj	212	11h	1.60
mandō, -āre, -āvī, -ātus	v	1	9	0.18
maneō, -ēre, mānsī, mānsus	v	2	7	0.38
mānēs, -ium (pl.)	n	4m	4h	0.17
manus, -ūs	n	4f	4b	1.68
mare, -is	n	3n	3c	0.79
marītus, -ī	n	2m	9	0.49
māter, -tris	n	3f	4a	1.01
māteria, -ae	n	1f	4j	0.22
mātūrus, -a, -um	adj	212	11f	0.17
maximē	adv	ind		<0.02
maximus, -a, -um	adj	212	11a	0.99
mē	pro			2.85
mēcum	adv	ind		0.34
medius, -a, -um	adj	212	11e	0.75
melior, -ius	adj	irr	11g	0.51
membrum, -ī	n	2n	4b	0.38
meminī, -isse, --	v	irr	4b	0.31
memor, -is	adj	3.1	4b	0.22
memoria, -ae	n	1f	4b	0.26
memorō, -āre, -āvī, -ātus	v	1	4b	0.25
mēns, mentis	n	3f	4b	0.95
mēnsa, -ae	n	1f	4i	0.17
mēnsis, -is	n	3m	2	0.16
mercātor, -oris	n	3m		0.04
mereō, -ēre, -uī, -itus	v	2	8	0.57
merus, -a, -um	adj	212	11g	0.20

messis, -is	n	3f	3e	0.16
metuō, -ere, -uī, --	v	3	4h	0.36
metus, -ūs	n	4m	4h	0.48
meus, -a, -um	adj	212		3.75
mihi	pro			3.49
mīles, -itis	n	3m	4f	0.97
mīlia, -ium (pl.)	n	3n	11b	0.49
minimē	adv	ind		<0.02
minimus, -a, -um	adj	212	11a	0.18
minister, -trī	n	2m	4a	0.21
minor, minus	adj	irr	11a	0.33
minus	adv	ind		0.50
mīror, -ārī, -ātus sum	v	1d	4g	0.47
mīrus, -a, -um	adj	212	4g	0.21
misceō, -ēre, miscuī, mixtus	v	2	9	0.38
miser, -era, -erum	adj	212	11h	0.74
mītis, -e	adj	3.2	11c	0.19
mittō, -ere, mīsī, missus	v	3	9	0.87
modo	adv	ind		0.97
modus, -ī	n	2m	4j	1.79
moenia, -ium (pl.)	n	3n	4f	0.20
mōlēs, -is	n	3f	4j	0.22
mollis, -e	adj	3.2	11c	0.44
moneō, -ēre, -uī, -itus	v	2	4e	0.32
mōns, montis	n	3m	3d	0.57
monumentum, -ī	n	2n	4h	0.17
mora, -ae	n	1f	2	0.20
morbus, -ī	n	2m	4h	0.18
morior, morī, mortuus sum	v	3d	4h	0.53
moror, -ārī, -ātus sum	v	1d	2	0.26
mors, -tis	n	3f	4h	1.36
mortālis, -e	adj	3.2	4h	0.46

mortuus, -a, -um	adj	212	4h	0.17
mōs, mōris	n	3m	4g	0.80
motus, motus	n	4m		0.23
moveō, -ēre, mōvī, mōtus	v	2	9	1.05
mox	adv	ind		0.37
mulier, -eris	n	3f	4a	0.17
multi	adj	212		0.41
multitūdō, -inis	n	3f	11b	0.24
multo	adv	ind		0.22
multum	adv	ind		0.51
multus, -a, -um	adj	212	11b	2.29
mundus, -a -um	adj	212		0.47
mundus, -ī	n	2m	3a	0.30
mūnus, -eris	n	3n	4g	0.71
mūrus, -ī	n	2m	4i	0.19
mūsa, -ae	n	1f		0.43
mūtō, -āre, -āvī, -ātus	v	1	10	0.38
nam	cnj	ind		1.64
namque	cnj	ind		0.30
narrō, -āre, -āvī, -ātus	v	1	4e	0.17
nāscor, -ī, nātus sum	v	3d	8	0.38
nauta, -ae	n	1m		0.09
nātūra, -ae	n	1f	4j	0.94
nātus, -ī	n	2m	8	0.81
nāvigō, -āre, -āvī, -ātus	v	1		0.07
nāvis, -is	n	3f	3c	0.25
nē	cnj	ind		2.17
ne (-ne)	adv	ind		0.90
nec (neque)	cnj	ind		6.78
necessarius -a -um	adj	212		0.21
necesse, necessis	adj	irr		0.20
necō, -āre, -āvī, -ātus	v	1		0.09

nectō, -ere, nex(u)ī, nexus	v	3	9	0.16
nefās	n	ind	4g	0.17
negligō, -ere, -lēxī, lēctus	v	3	5	0.18
negō, -āre, -āvī, -ātus	v	1	4e	0.41
negotium, -ī	n	2n		0.24
nēmō (nūllīus, nēminī, nēminem, nūllō)	pro		4j	0.51
nemus, -oris	n	3n	3e	0.36
nepōs, -ōtis	n	3m	4a	0.16
neque	adv	ind		2.13
nesciō, -īre, -īvī, -ītus	v	4	4c	0.33
nēve (neu)	cnj	ind		0.18
niger, -gra, -grum	adj	212	11d	0.37
nihil or nīl (indecl.)	pro		4j	1.28
nil	n	ind		0.29
nimius, -a, -um	adj	212		0.26
nisī (nisi)	cnj	ind		0.91
niteō, -ēre, -uī, --	v	2	8	0.22
nitidus, -a, -um	adj	212	8	0.17
niveus, -a, -um	adj	212	3a	0.22
nix, nivis	n	3f	3a	0.24
nōbilis, -e	adj	3.2	11g	0.38
nōbīs	pro			0.89
noceō, -ēre, -uī, -itus	v	2	5	0.28
nocturnus, -a, -um	adj	212	2	0.22
nōlō, nōlle, nōluī, --	v	irr	4c	0.30
nōmen, -inis	n	3n	4j	1.28
nōn	adv	ind		9.38
nōndum	adv	ind		0.18
nonne	adv	ind		0.08
nōs	pro			0.79
nōscō, -ere, nōvī, nōtus	v	3	4c	0.57
noster, -tra, -trum	adj	212		2.65

omnis, -e	adj	3.2	11b	5.45
opera, -ae	n	1f		0.23
oportet, -tēre, -tuit, --	v	2		0.16
oppidum, -ī	n	2n		0.34
opprimō, -ere, -pressī, -pressus	v	3	10	0.16
oppugnō, -āre, -āvī, -ātus	v	1		0.06
ops, opis	n	3f	4i	0.59
optimus, -a, -um	adj	212	11g	0.31
optō, -āre, -āvī, -ātus	v	1	4g	0.30
opus, -eris	n	3n	4i	1.00
ōra, -ae	n	1f	3c	0.17
ōrātiō, -ōnis	n	3f	4e	0.18
ōrātor, -ōris	n	3m	4e	0.16
orbis, -is	n	3m	3a	0.91
ōrdō, -inis	n	3m	4j	0.40
orior, orīrī, ortus sum	v	3d	7	0.65
ōrnō, -āre, -āvī, -ātus	v	1	6	0.21
ōrō, -āre, -āvī, -ātus	v	1		0.21
ōs, ōris	n	3n	4b	0.32
os, ossis	n	3n		1.09
ōsculum, -ī	n	2n	4b	0.20
ostendō, -ere, -tendī, -tensus	v	3	10	0.29
ōtium, -ī	n	2n	4i	0.29
paene	adv	ind		0.21
palleō, -ēre, -uī, --	v	2	8	0.16
pandō, -ere, pandī, passus	v	3	9	0.21
pār, paris	adj	3.1	11b	0.46
paratus -a -um	adj	212		0.23
parcō, -ere, parcuī, parsūs	v	3	8	0.40
parēns, -entis	n	3mf	4a	0.79
pareō, -ēre, parui, partitus	v	2		0.17
pariō, -ere, peperī, partus	v	3-io	4a	0.37

146

pariter	adv	ind	11b	0.24
parō, -āre, -āvī, -ātus	v	1	10	0.52
pars, partis	n	3f	4j	1.48
parum	adv	ind	11a	0.23
parvus, -a, -um	adj	212	11a	0.65
pateō, -ēre, -uī, --	v	2	8	0.38
pater, -tris	n	3m	4a	1.20
patior, -ī, passus sum	v	3d	4h	0.46
patria, -ae	n	1f	4a	0.62
patrius, -a, -um	adj	212		0.23
paucus, -a, -um	adj	212	11b	0.46
paulo	adv	ind		0.22
paulus, -a, -um	adj	212	11b	0.31
pauper, -eris	n	3m	4a	0.17
pāx, pācis	n	3f	4f	0.39
pectus, -oris	n	3n	4b	0.84
pecūnia, -ae	n	1f	3f	0.22
pecus, -udis	n	3f	3f	0.22
pecus, -oris	n	3n	3f	0.20
pelagus, -ī	n	2n	3c	0.28
pellō, -ere, pepulī, pulsus	v	3	9	0.20
pendeō, -ēre, pependī, --	v	2	9	0.18
pendō, -ere, pependī, pēnsus	v	3	9	0.26
penetrō, -āre, -āvī, -ātus	v	1	7	0.17
per (+Ak)	prp	ind		3.79
peragō, -ere, -ēgī, -āctus	v	3	9	0.18
perdō, -ere, -didī, -ditus	v	3	5	0.32
pereō, -īre, -iī, -itus	v	irr	7	0.55
perferō, -ferre, -tulī, -lātus	v	irr	9	0.18
perīculum, -ī	n	2n	4f	0.53
permittō, -ere, -mīsī, -missus	v	3	9	0.30
perpetuus, -a, -um	adj	212	11f	0.18

persuādeō, -ēre, persuasi, persuasus	v	2	0.10
perterritus, -a, -um	adj	212	<0.02
pertineō, -ēre, -tinuī, --	v	2	9	0.17
perveniō, -īre, -vēnī, -ventus	v	4	7	0.31
pēs, pedis	n	3m	4b	0.83
petō, -ere, -īvī (-iī), -ītus	v	3	7	1.00
philosophia, -ae	n	1f		0.21
pietās, -ātis	n	3f	11g	0.24
pingō, -ere, pīnxī, pictus	v	3	10	0.22
pinguis, -e	adj	3.2	11d	0.18
pius, -a, -um	adj	212	11g	0.49
placeō, -ēre, -uī, -itus	v	2	4g	0.49
placidus, -a, -um	adj	212	4g	0.27
plaudō, -ere, plausī, plausus	v	3	4g	0.16
plebes, -ei	n	5f		0.35
plēnus, -a, -um	adj	212	11c	0.44
plerusque -aque -umque	adj	212		0.24
plūrimus, -a, -um	adj	212	11b	0.28
plūs, plūris	adj	irr	11b	0.83
pōculum, -ī	n	2n	4i	0.17
poena, -ae	n	1f	4h	0.38
poēta, -ae	n	1m	4e	0.33
poetntia, -ae	n	1f		0.22
polus, -ī	n	2m	3a	0.19
pondus, -eris	n	3n	4j	0.35
pōnō, -ere, posuī, positus	v	3	9	0.91
pontus, -ī	n	2m	3c	0.42
populus, -ī	n	2m	4a	0.84
porta, -ae	n	1f	9	0.27
portō, -āre, -āvī, -ātus	v	1		0.13
portus, -ūs	n	4m		0.17
poscō, -ere, poposcī, --	v	3		0.18

possum, posse, potuī	v	irr	8	3.88
post (+Ak)	prp	ind		0.78
posteā	adv	ind		0.14
posterus, -a, -um	adj	212		0.20
postquam	cnj	ind		0.43
postrīdiā	adv	ind		<0.02
potēns, potentis	adj	3.1	8	0.24
potestās, -ātis	n	3f	8	0.16
potis, -e	adj	3.2	8	0.55
potius	adv	ind		0.33
praebeō, -ēre, -buī, -bitus	v	2	9	0.27
praeceptum, -ī	n	2n		0.22
praecipiō, -cipere, -cepī, -ceptus	v	3		0.26
praecipuus, -a, -um	adj	212	11g	0.17
praeda, -ae	n	1f	4f	0.16
praeferō, -ferre, -tulī, -lātus	v	irr	9	0.16
praemium, -ī	n	2n	4g	0.22
praesidium, -ī	n	2n	4f	0.18
praestō, -stāre, -stitī, -stitus	v	1	7	0.40
praeter (+Ak)	prp	ind		0.19
praintereā	adv	ind		0.22
praetereō, -īre, -iī, -itus	v	irr	7	0.21
precor, -ārī, -ātus sum	v	1d	4e	0.32
premō, -ere, pressī, pressus	v	3	10	0.55
pretium, -ī	n	2n	4i	0.22
prex, precis	n	3f	4e	0.23
prīmō	adv	ind		0.18
primum	adv	ind		0.60
prīmus, -a, -um	adj	212	11b	2.20
prīnceps, -ipis	n	3m	4a	0.45
prīncipium, -ī	n	2n	4a	0.19
prior, prius	adj	irr	11b	0.27

prīscus, -a, -um	adj	212	11f	0.17
prius	adv	ind		0.20
prō (+Ab)	prp	ind		0.88
probō, -āre, -āvī, -ātus	v	1	4g	0.30
prōcēdō, -ēre, -cessī, -cessus	v	2	7	0.19
procul	adv	ind		0.43
prōdō, -ere, -didī, -ditus	v	3	9	0.25
proelium, -ī	n	2n	4f	0.56
proficiscor, proficisci, profectus sum	v	3d		0.24
prohibeō, -ēre, -uī, -itus	v	2	9	0.18
prōiciō, -ere, -iēcī, -iectus	v	3	9	0.20
prōlēs, -is	n	3f	4a	0.22
prōmittō, -ere, -mīsī, -missus	v	3	9	0.44
prope	adv	ind		0.36
properō, -āre, -āvī, -ātus	v	1	7	0.18
propior -pius	adj	irr		0.55
prōpōnō, -ere, -posuī, -positus	v	3	9	0.38
proprius, -a, -um	adj	212	11e	0.34
propter (+Ak)	prp	ind		0.33
prōsum, prōdesse, prōfuī, profuturus	v	irr	8	0.18
prōtinus	adv	ind		0.58
provincia, -ae	n	1f		0.38
proximus, -a, -um	adj	212		0.91
pūblicus, -a, -um	adj	212	11e	0.20
pudeō, -ēre, -uī, -itus	v	2		0.20
pudor, -ōris	n	3m	4h	0.26
puella, -ae	n	1f	4a	0.99
puer, puerī	n	2m	4a	1.03
pugna, -ae	n	1f		0.31
pūgnō, -āre, -āvī, -ātus	v	1	5	0.30
pulcher -chra -chrum	adj	212	11d	0.41
pūniō, -īre, -iī, -itus	v	4		0.09

quisquis, quidquid / quicquid (subst., quodquod, adj.)	pro			0.67
quō	adv	ind		0.16
quod	cnj	ind		1.20
quomodo	adv	ind		0.26
quondam	adv	ind		0.34
quoniam	cnj	ind		0.34
quoque	adv	ind		1.25
quot	adj	irr	11b	0.16
quotiē(n)s	adv	ind		0.23
rāmus, -ī	n	2m	3e	0.19
rapidus, -a, -um	adj	212	11f	0.22
rapiō, -ere, rapuī, raptus	v	3-io	9	0.59
rārus, -a, -um	adj	212	11b	0.30
ratiō, -ōnis	n	3f	4b	0.76
ratis, -is	n	3f	3c	0.23
recipiō, -ere, -cēpī, -ceptus	v	3-io	9	0.26
rēctus, -a, -um	adj	212	10	0.26
reddō, -ere, -didī, -ditus	v	3	9	0.57
redeō, -īre, -iī, -itus	v	irr	7	0.59
referō, referre, rettulī, relātum	v	irr	9	0.87
rēgīna, -ae	n	1f		0.11
regiō, -ōnis	n	3f	10	0.18
rēgius, -a, -um	adj	212	10	0.19
rēgnō, -āre, -āvī, -ātus	v	1	10	0.17
rēgnum, -ī	n	2n	10	0.55
regō, -ere, rēxī, rēctus	v	3	10	0.39
regredior, regredī, regressus sum	v	3d		0.06
religiō, -ōnis	n	3f	1	0.16
relinquō, -ere, -līquī, -lictus	v	3	9	0.68
reliquus -a -um	adj	212	9	0.39
reor, rērī, ratus sum	v	2d	4c	0.18

reperiō, -īre, repperī, repertus	v	4	9	0.28
repeto, -ere, -īvī (-iī), -ītus	v	3	7	0.22
rēs, reī	n	5f	4j	3.77
resistō, -ere, restiti, --	v	3		0.17
respiciō, -ere, -exī, -ectus	v	3-io	4c	0.29
respondeō, -ēre, -spondī, -spōnsus	v	2	4e	0.19
respublica	n	5f		0.67
retineō, -ēre, -tinuī, retentus	v	2	9	0.27
revertō, -ere, -i, --	v	3		0.18
revocō, -āre, -āvī, -ātus	v	1	4e	0.24
rēx, rēgis	n	3m	10	1.02
rīdeō, -ēre, rīsī, rīsus	v	2	4g	0.33
rīpa, -ae	n	1f	3c	0.34
rogō, -āre, -āvī, -ātus	v	1	4e	0.31
rogus, -ī	n	2m	4h	0.22
rōmanus -a -um	adj	212		0.95
rosa, -ae	n	1f	3e	0.28
rota, -ae	n	1f	4j	0.16
rubeō, -ēre, -uī, --	v	2	8	0.16
rudis, -e	adj	3.2	11h	0.22
ruīna, -ae	n	1f	7	0.17
rumpō, -ere, rupi, ruptus	v	3		0.34
ruō, -ere, ruī, rutus	v	3	7	0.18
rūrsus (rūrsum)	adv	ind		0.31
rūs, rūris	n	3n	3d	0.31
rūsticus, -a, -um	adj	212	3d	0.16
sacer, -cra, -crum	adj	212	11g	0.91
sacrum, -ī	n	2n		0.21
saeculum, -ī	n	2n	2	0.43
saepe	adv	ind		1.13
saevus, -a, -um	adj	212	11h	0.48
salūs, -ūtis	n	3f	4g	0.27

salūto, -āre, -āvī, -ātus	v	1		0.06
sānctus, -a, -um	adj	212	11g	0.36
sanguis, -inis	n	3m	4b	0.50
sānus, -a, -um	adj	212	11g	0.16
sapiens sapientis	n	3m		0.51
sapientia, -ae	n	1f		0.27
satis	adv	ind		0.73
saxum, -ī	n	2n	3d	0.38
scelestus, -a, -um	adj	212		0.03
scelus, -eris	n	3n	4h	0.31
scīlicet	adv	ind		0.16
sciō, scīre, scīvī (sciī), scītus	v	4	4c	0.71
scrībō, -ere, scrīpsī, scrīptus	v	3	4c	0.68
sē or sēsē	pro			2.67
secundus, -a, -um	adj	212	7	0.42
sēcūrus, -a, -um	adj	212	4g	0.24
sed	cnj	ind		4.28
sedeō, -ēre, sēdī, sessus	v	2	7	0.26
sēdēs, -is	n	3f	7	0.40
semel	adv	ind		0.21
sēmen, -inis	n	3n	3e	0.17
semper	adv	ind		1.11
senātor, -tōris	n	3m		0.09
senātus, -ūs	n	4m	4a	0.26
senectūs, -ūtis	n	3f	4a	0.16
senex, -is	n	3mf	4a	0.66
sēnsus, -ūs	n	4m	4c	0.19
sententia, -ae	n	1f	4c	0.19
sentiō, -īre, sēnsī, sēnsus	v	4	4c	0.47
sepulcrum, -ī	n	2n	4h	0.35
sequor, -ī, secūtus sum	v	3d	7	0.80
serēnus, -a, -um	adj	212	11g	0.19

sermō, -ōnis	n	3m	4e	0.37
sertum, -ī	n	2n	3e	0.17
serviō, -īre, -īvī, -ītus	v	4	6	0.22
servō, -āre, -āvī, -ātus	v	1	6	0.43
servus, -ī	n	2m	6	0.35
sese	pro			0.38
seu	cnj	ind		0.64
sī	cnj	ind		4.69
sibi	pro			1.13
sīc	adv	ind		1.75
sīcut (sīcutī)	adv	ind		0.18
sīdus, -eris	n	3n	3a	0.63
sīgnum, -ī	n	2n	4f	0.73
sileō, -ēre, -uī, --	v	2	4e	0.17
silva, -ae	n	1f	3e	0.57
similis, -e	adj	3.2		0.38
simul	adv	ind		0.70
simulac, simulatque	adv	ind		<0.02
sine (+Ab)	prp	ind		1.24
singulus -a -um	adj	212		0.29
sinister, -tra, -trum	adj	212	4b	0.16
sinō, -ere, sīvī, situs	v	3	4c	0.16
sinus, -ūs	n	4m	3c	0.38
sīve (seu)	cnj	ind		0.38
socius, -ī	n	2m	4a	0.34
sōl, sōlis	n	3m	3a	0.87
soleō, -ēre, solitus sum	v	2sd	4c	0.57
sollicitus, -a, -um	adj	212	11h	0.19
solum	adv	ind		0.22
sōlus, -a, -um	adj	212-ius	11b	1.27
solvō, -ere, solvī, solūtus	v	3	10	0.61
somnium, -ī	n	2n	2	0.18

155

somnus, -ī	n	2m	2	0.65
sonō, -āre, -nuī, -nitus	v	1	4e	0.43
sonus, -ī	n	2m	4e	0.18
soror, -ōris	n	3f	4a	0.36
sors, sortis	n	3f	1	0.26
spargō, -ere, -rsī, -rsus	v	3	9	0.29
spatium, -ī	n	2n	4j	0.30
speciēs, -ēī	n	5f	4b	0.37
spectō, -āre, -āvī, -ātus	v	1	4c	0.25
spernō, -ere, sprēvī, sprētus	v	3	4h	0.18
spērō, -āre, -āvī, -ātus	v	1	4d	0.25
spēs, -eī	n	5f	4d	0.55
spīritus, -ūs	n	4m	8	0.21
spīrō, -āre, -āvī, -ātus	v	1	8	0.20
statim	adv	ind		0.26
statuō, -ere, -uī, -ūtus	v	3	4c	0.16
stēlla, -ae	n	1f	3a	0.26
sternō, -ere, strāvī, strātus	v	3	9	0.23
stō, stāre, stetī, status	v	1	7	0.82
studium, -ī	n	2n	4g	0.54
stultus, -a, -um	adj	212		0.14
sub (+Ak/Ab)	prp	ind		1.24
subeō, -īre, -iī, -itus	v	irr	7	0.41
subitō	adv	ind		0.16
sublīmis, -e	adj	3.2	11e	0.24
sui soi	pro			6.28
sum, esse, fuī, futūrus	v	irr	8	23.16
summus -a -um	adj	212		0.94
sūmō, -ere, sūmpsī, sūmptus	v	3	9	0.29
super (+Ak/Ab)	prp	ind		0.46
superbus, -a, -um	adj	212		0.31
superior, -ius	adj	irr		0.18

superō, -āre, -āvī, -ātus	v	1		0.26
supersum, superesse, superfuī, superfuturus	v	irr	8	0.29
superus	adj	212		1.18
supplicium, -ī	n	2n		0.28
suprā (+Ak)	prp	ind		0.23
suprēmus, -a, -um	adj	212		0.19
surgō, -ere, surrēxī, surrēctus	v	3	7	0.36
sustineō, -ēre, sustinuī, sustentus	v	2	9	0.25
suus, -a, -um	adj	212		3.78
taberna, -ae	n	1f		0.03
taceō, -ēre, -uī, -itus	v	2	4e	0.20
tacitus, -a, -um	adj	212	4e	0.21
tālis, -e	adj	3.2		0.51
tam	adv	ind		1.03
tamen	cnj	ind		2.10
tamquam	cnj	ind		0.35
tandem	cnj	ind		0.24
tangō, -ere, tetigī, tāctus	v	3	7	0.24
tantum	adv	ind		0.73
tantus, -a, -um	adj	212	11a	1.80
tardus, -a, -um	adj	212	11f	0.29
taurus, -ī	n	2m	3f	0.21
tē	pro			3.28
tēctum, -ī	n	2n	10	0.34
tēcum	pro			0.26
tegō, -ere, tēxī, tēctus	v	3	10	0.23
tellūs, -ūris	n	3f	3d	0.47
tēlum, -ī	n	2n	4f	0.35
temperō, -āre, -āvī, -ātus	v	1	10	0.19
tempestas -tātis	n	3f		0.23
templum, -ī	n	2n	1	0.43

temptō, -āre, -āvī, -ātus	v	1	0.26
tempus, -oris	n	3n	2	2.01
tendō, -ere, tetendī, tentus	v	3	10	0.19
tenebrae, -ārum	n	1f	2	0.29
teneō, -ēre, tenuī, tentus	v	2	9	1.10
tener, -era, -erum	adj	212	11c	0.56
tentō, -āre, -āvī, -ātus	v	1		0.35
tenuis, -e	adj	3.2	11a	0.19
ter	adv	ind	11b	0.18
tergum, -ī	n	2n	4b	0.37
terō, -ere, trīvī, trītus	v	3	10	0.22
terra, -ae	n	1f	3d	1.51
terreō, -ēre, -uī, -itus	v	2	4h	0.18
terror, -ōris	n	3m	4h	0.18
tertius, -a, -um	adj	212	11b	0.22
thalamus, -ī	n	2m	4i	0.20
tibi	pro			2.77
timeō, -ēre, -uī, --	v	2	4h	0.52
timor, -ōris	n	3m	4h	0.27
titulus, -ī	n	2m	4e	0.16
tollō, -ere, sustulī, sublātus	v	3	9	0.38
torqueō, -ēre, torsi, tortus	v	2		0.24
torreō, -ēre, torruī, tostus	v	2	10	0.18
torus, -ī	n	2m	4i	0.33
tot	adj	irr	11b	0.43
tōtus, -a, -um	adj	212-ius	11b	1.40
trādō, -ere, -didī, -ditus	v	3	9	0.34
trahō, -ere, trāxī, tractus	v	3	9	0.36
trāiciō, -ere, -iēcī, -iectus	v	3-io	9	0.20
trans (+ Ac)	prp	ind		0.14
trānseō, -īre, -iī, -itus	v	irr	7	0.24
trēs, trēs, tria	adj	irr	11b	0.37

ūtor, ūtī, ūsus sum	v	3d	6	0.37
utrum	adv	ind		0.24
uxor, -ōris	n	3f	9	0.34
vacō, -āre, -āvī, -ātus	v	1	8	0.19
vacuus, -a, -um	adj	212	8	0.24
vadum, -ī	n	2n	7	0.21
vagus, -a, -um	adj	212	7	0.35
valeō, -ēre, -uī, -itūrus	v	2	4g	0.54
validus, -a, -um	adj	212	4g	0.16
vānus, -a, -um	adj	212	11c	0.19
varius, -a, -um	adj	212		0.51
vāstus, -a, -um	adj	212	11h	0.16
vātēs, -is	n	3mf	1	0.55
ve (-ve)	cnj	ind		0.87
vehementer	adv	ind		0.09
vehō, -ere, vēxī, vectus	v	3	9	0.38
vel	adv	ind		1.13
vēlum, -ī	n	2n	3c	0.17
velut (velutī)	adv	ind		0.38
vendō, -ere, vendidi, venditus	v	3		0.12
venēnum, -ī	n	2n	4h	0.16
veniō, -īre, vēnī, ventus	v	4	7	2.01
ventus, -ī	n	2m	3a	0.60
vēr, vēris	n	3n	2	0.71
verbum, -ī	n	2n	4e	0.25
vereor, -ērī, veritus sum	v	2d	4h	0.88
vērō	adv	ind	11g	0.18
versō, -āre, -āvī, -ātus	v	1	9	0.83
versus, -ūs	n	4m	4e	0.21
vertex (or vortex), -icis	n	3m	9	0.44
vertō, -ere, -rtī, -rsus	v	3	9	0.20
verum, -ī	n	2n		0.26

volō, -āre, -āvī, -ātus	v	1		0.24
volō, velle, voluī, --	v	irr	4c	1.53
volucris, -is	n	3f	4c	0.34
voluntās, -ātis	n	3f	4c	0.18
voluptās, -ātis	n	3f	4c	0.28
volvō, -ere, volvī, volūtus	v	3	9	0.17
vōs vestrum	pro			0.54
vōtum, -ī	n	2n	1	0.63
vōx, vōcis	n	3f	4e	0.81
vulgō, -āre, -āvī, -ātus	v	1	4a	0.17
vulgus, -ī	n	2n	4a	0.20
vulnerō, -āre, -āvī, -ātus	v	1		0.07
vulnus, -eris	n	3n	4h	0.38
vultus, -ūs	n	4m	4b	0.59

CHAPTER 5

ENDINGS & PARADIGMS

This chapter presents a summary of the inflected forms that may be taken by the nouns, adjectives and verbs within the vocabulary. This summary is not, by any stretch of the imagination, a grammar, but it should prove helpful as a quick reference to students who wish to recite or write out full declensions or conjugations. The pages can also be used to review inflected endings as an aid to recognising patterns within the various grammatical categories.

Within each paradigm, the lexical forms of the terms are highlighted for quick recognition.

NOUNS

I DECLENSION NOUNS (-*a*, -*ae*)

I Dcl nouns are overwhelmingly F with a few M nouns, usually referring to an occupation such as *farmer* or *poet*. The endings for both the M and the F are identical:

	Singular	*Plural*			Thus: worry
Nm	-a	-ae	Nm	cūra	cūrae
Ac	-am	-ās	Ac	cūram	cūrās
Gn	-ae	-ārum	Gn	cūrae	cūrārum
Dt	-ae	-īs	Dt	cūrae	cūrīs
Ab	-ā	-īs	Ab	cūrā	cūrīs

II DECLENSION NOUNS

Most nouns of the II Dcl are M, though the Nt are used more frequently than the more numerous M examples; Feminine nouns of the II Dcl are more rare. M and F nouns take identical endings. The Nt endings differ slightly, and only in the Nom and Acc.

A. *Masc & Fem endings* (-*us*, -*ī*)

	Singular	*Plural*			Thus: slave
Nm	-us	-ī	Nm	servus	servī
Ac	-um	-ōs	Ac	servum	servōs
Gn	-ī	-ōrum	Gn	servī	servōrum
Dt	-ō	-īs	Dt	servō	servīs
Ab	-ō	-īs	Ab	servō	servīs

II Dcl nouns with stems that end in -*r* or in -*er* (all are M) will drop the -*us* in the Nom S. Thus:

ager, agrī	magister, -trī	puer, puerī
liber, librī	minister, ministrī	vir, virī

They are otherwise regular: remove the -*ī* from the Gen S, as given in the Lexicon, and attach the endings as usual. Note that some nouns have -*er*- as the stem, while others take only -*r*-. The student must learn the Nom S and the Gen S by heart, and take care not to confuse these terms with III Dcl M nouns.

B. Neut endings: -um, -ī

	Singular	Plural			Thus: word
Nm	-um	-a	Nm	verbum	verba
Ac	-um	-a	Ac	verbum	verba
Gn	-ī	-ōrum	Gn	verbī	verbōrum
Dt	-ō	-īs	Dt	verbō	verbīs
Ab	-ō	-īs	Ab	verbō	verbīs

III Declension Nouns

Nouns of the III Dcl have no regular ending for the Nom S. There are regular endings for all other cases. Terms are split fairly evenly between M and F words. There is a sizeable minority of Nt terms as well. The M and F endings are identical. Nt endings differ from the M and F endings only in the Nom and Acc.

A. Masc & Fem endings: --, -is

	Singular	Plural			Thus: lion
Nm	--	-ēs	Nm	leō	leōnēs
Ac	-em	-ēs	Ac	leōnem	leōnēs
Gn	-is	-(i)um	Gn	leōnis	leōnum
Dt	-ī	-ibus	Dt	leōnī	leōnibus
Ab	-e	-ibus	Ab	leōne	leōnibus

Nota Bene: Gen Pl endings in the III Decl may be either *-um* or *-ium*. There is no simple rule that assists the student here. Variations are more common in the M and F, less common in the Nt, but note *mare* with *marium* in the Gn Pl.

B. Neuter Endings: --, -is

	Singular	Plural			Thus: heart
Nm	--	-a	Nm	cor	corda
Ac	--	-a	Ac	cor	corda
Gn	-is	-um	Gn	cordis	cordum
Dt	-ī	-ibus	Dt	cordī	cordibus
Ab	-e	-ibus	Ab	corde	cordibus

IV DECLENSION NOUNS

Most nouns of the IV Dcl are M, a few are F or Nt. The M and F nouns generally take identical endings, though F nouns will occasionally take -ō as the Dat or Abl S. The Nt endings differ from either of these.

A. Masc & Fem endings: -us, -ūs

	Singular	Plural			Thus: fear
Nm	-us	-ūs	Nm	metus	metūs
Ac	-um	-ūs	Ac	metum	metūs
Gn	-ūs	-uum	Gn	metūs	metuum
Dt	-uī	-ibus	Dt	metuī	metibus
Ab	-ū	-ibus	Ab	metū	metibus

B. Neuter endings: -ū, -ūs

	Singular	Plural			Thus: horn
Nm	-ū	-ua	Nm	cornū	cornua
Ac	-ū	-ua	Ac	cornū	cornua
Gn	-ūs	-uum	Gn	cornūs	cornuum
Dt	-ū	-ibus	Dt	cornū	cornibus
Ab	-ū	-ibus	Ab	cornū	cornibus

166

V DECLENSION NOUNS

There are very few V Dcl nouns, and most of these are F. The only exceptions are the M words diēs and merīdiēs, and even these may be F when referencing a specific day as opposed to "some day" or "a day." Furthermore, the forms listed below have occasional exceptions. Most notably, the usual -*ēī* becomes -*eī* after a consonant. Thus: reī rather than rēī. With the exceptions of diēs and rēs, these terms are not often found in the plural.

	Singular	*Plural*		Thus:	sharp edge
Nm	-ēs	-ēs	Nm	aciēs	aciēs
Ac	-em	-ēs	Ac	aciem	aciēs
Gn	-ēī	-ērum	Gn	aciēī	aciērum
Dt	-ēī	-ēbus	Dt	aciēī	aciēbus
Ab	-ē	-ēbus	Ab	aciē	aciēbus

After a consonant:

	trust			thing	
Nm	fidēs	fidēs	Nm	rēs	rēs
Ac	fidem	fidēs	Ac	rem	rēs
Gn	fideī	fidērum	Gn	reī	rērum
Dt	fideī	fidēbus	Dt	reī	rēbus
Ab	fidē	fidēbus	Ab	rē	rēbus

ADJECTIVES

REGULAR I & II DECLENSION
[2-1-2 ADJECTIVES]

These adjectives will assume II Dcl endings when they modify a masculine or neuter noun. They take I Dcl endings when modifying a feminine noun.

	Singular			Plural		
	M	**F**	**Nt**	**M**	**F**	**Nt**
Nm	-us*	-a	-um	-ī	-ae	-a
Ac	-um	-am	-um	-ōs	-ās	-a
Gn	-ī	-ae	-ī	-ōrum	-ārum	-ōrum
Dt	-ō	-ae	-ō	-īs		
Ab		-ā				

*Some M adjectives end in -r or -er in the Nom S. Note that some of those ending in -er will keep the -e- as they decline while others will drop it in the declension

Thus: true, genuine

	Singular			Plural		
	M	**F**	**Nt**	**M**	**F**	**Nt**
Nm	vērus	vēra	vērum	vērī	vērae	vēra
Ac	vērum	vēram	vērum	vērōs	vērās	vēra
Gn	vērī	vērae	vērī	vērōrum	vērārum	vērōrum
Dt	vērō	vērae	vērō	vērīs		
Ab		vērā				

"IRREGULAR"
–*īus* GEN 2-1-2 ADJECTIVES

There are only nine of these. In all cases of the plural, they are regular 2-1-2 adjectives.

| | Singular | | | Plural | Other Irregular |
	M	F	Nt	M, F, Nt	212 Adjectives
Nm	alius alter nullus neuter	alia altera nulla neutra	aliud alterum nullum neutrum		
Ac	alium alterum nullum neutrum	aliam alteram nullam neutram	aliud alterum nullum neutrum		sōlus tōtus ullus ūnus } All follow the pattern of nullus
Gn	alīus alterīus nullīus neutrīus	alīus alterīus nullīus neutrīus	alīus alterīus nullīus neutrīus	Regular in all plurals	
Dt	aliī alterī nullī neutrī	aliī alterī nullī neutrī	aliī alterī nullī neutrī		uter: follows neuter
Ab	aliō alterō nullō neutrō	aliā alterā nullā neutrā	aliō alterō nullō neutrō		

169

3.1 ADJECTIVES
(III DECLENSION, SINGLE TERMINATION)

One Nom S ending covers all genders and is generally unpredictable. Furthermore, these words usually have stem changes. Thus, the lexicon provides the Nom S, and then the Gen S, which reveals the stem (by removing the *-is*). Note that a very few, rare, 3.1 adjectives will take *-e* in the Abl S and and will drop the *-i-* in the Nom and Acc Nt Pl as well as in all Gen Pl. The words *vetus* (old) and *pauper* (used as an adjective) follow this pattern.

Note, also, that the present participle of all verbs may be viewed as a 3.1 adjective, though when used as a substantive, the participles take an *-e* in the Abl S.

	Singular		Plural	
	M/F	**Nt**	**M/F**	**Nt**
Nm	--		-ēs	-ia
Ac	-em	--	-ēs	-ia
Gn	-is		-ium	
Dt	-ī		-ibus	
Ab				

Thus: diligent

	Singular		Plural	
	M/F	**Nt**	**M/F**	**Nt**
Nm	dīligens		dīligentēs	dīligentia
Ac	dīligentem	dīligens	dīligentēs	dīligentia
Gn	dīligentis		dīligentium	
Dt	dīligentī		dīligentibus	
Ab				

3.2 ADJECTIVES
(III DECLENSION, TWO TERMINATIONS)

These adjectives have one ending in the Nom that covers both M and F nouns (-*is*), and a second ending (-*e*) that is for Nt nouns. The two terminations are given in the lexicon.

	Singular		*Plural*	
	M / F	*Nt*	*M / F*	*Nt*
Nm	-is	-e	-ēs	-ia
Ac	-em	-e	-ēs, -īs*	-ia
Gn	-is		-ium	
Dt	-ī		-ibus	
Ab				

*Either ending may be found in the Acc Pl.

Thus: sweet

	Singular		*Plural*	
	M / F	*Nt*	*M / F*	*Nt*
Nm	dulcis	dulce	dulcēs	dulcia
Ac	dulcem	dulce	dulcēs	dulcia
Gn	dulcis		dulcium	
Dt	dulcī		dulcibus	
Ab				

3.3 ADJECTIVES
(III DECLENSION, THREE TERMINATIONS)

These adjectives have distinct endings for each gender in the Nom. The three terminations are given in the lexicon.

	Singular			*Plural*		
	M	**F**	**Nt**	**M**	**F**	**Nt**
Nm	-er	-ris	-re	-ēs	-ēs	-ia
Ac	-em	-em	-re	-ēs, -īs*	-ēs	-ia
Gn	-is			-ium		
Dt	-ī			-ibus		
Ab						

*Either ending may be found in the Acc S.

Thus: swift

	Singular			*Plural*		
	M	**F**	**Nt**	**M**	**F**	**Nt**
Nm	celer	celeris	celere	celerēs	celerēs	celeria
Ac	celerem	celerem	celere	celerēs	celerēs	celeria
Gn	celeris			celerium		
Dt	celerī			celeribus		
Ab						

VERBS
I. PRINCIPLE PARTS

Verbs are learned with four principle parts: the first person singular present active indicative form, the infinitive, the first person singular perfect active indicative, and the perfect passive participle. Thus:

1st Principle Part	2nd Principle Part	3rd Principle Part	4th Principle Part
(1st S Pr Ac Ind)	(Pr Ac Infinitive)	(1st S Prf Ac Ind)	(Prf Pass Particip)
doceō	docēre	docuī	doctus
I teach	*to teach*	*I taught*	*having been taught*

The principle parts provide the stems or building blocks for constructing the whole range of fundamental tenses. The combination of the first principle part and the infinitive ending of the second principle part identifies the conjugation to which the verb belongs:

I Conj		II Conj		III Conj		IV Conj		III / IV Conj*	
1 pp	Inf	1 pp	Inf	1 pp	Inf	1 pp	Inf	1 pp	Inf
-ō	-āre	-eō	-ēre	-ō	-ere	-iō	-īre	-iō	-ere

*These verbs are sometimes referred to as "III Conjugation -iō verbs," and behave as regular III Conj verbs in the Inf and Perf tense. However, they take IV Conjugation forms in the Present, Future, and Imperfect tenses.

1st Principle Part. The present stem is used to form the present, imperfect and future tenses for the indicative as well as the present subjunctive. This is true of both the active and passive voices. In short, here are the fundamental tenses based upon the stem of the 1st Principle Part:

Pr Ac, Ind & Sbj	*Imprf Ac Ind*	*Fut Ac Ind*
Pr Pass, Ind & Sbj	*Imperf Pass Ind*	*Fut Pass Ind*

2nd Principle Part. The present active infinitive serves as the stem of the imperfect subjunctive, both active and passive.

3rd Principle Part. The perfect stem is used to form a variety of tenses: the Perfect, Pluperfect and Future Perfect tenses for the Active Indicative; the perfect and pluperfect active subjunctive. In short, here are the fundamental tenses based upon the 3rd Principle Part:

Prf Ac Ind & Sbj	*Plprf Ac Ind & Sbj*	*Fut Prf Ac Ind*

4th Principle Part. The Perfect Passive Participle serves as the base for the perfect, pluperfect, future perfect passive indicative, as well as the perfect and pluperfect passive subjunctive:

Prf Ps Ind & Sbj	Plprf Ps Ind & Sbj	FutPrf Ps Ind

As part of the verb, the participle always occurs in the Nom, but agrees with the subject in number and gender; S: -us, -a -um; Pl: -ī, -ae, -a.

The use of the principle parts as building blocks for the various fundamental tenses is seen in the following chart:

	Indicative	1st	2nd	3rd	4th	Subjunctive	1st	2nd	3rd	4th
A c t i v e	Pr Ac Ind	x				Pr Ac Sbj	x			
	Imprf Ac Ind	x				Imprf Ac Sbj		x		
	Fut Ac Ind	x				--				
	Prf Ac Ind			x		Prf Ac Sbj			x	
	Pluprf Ac Ind			x		Pluprf Ac Sbj			x	
	FutPrf Ac Ind			x		--				
P a s s i v e	Pr Ps Ind	x				Pr Ps Sbj	x			
	Imprf Ps Ind	x				Imprf Ps Sbj		x		
	Fut Ps Ind	x				--				
	Prf Ps Ind				x	Prf Ps Sbj				x
	Pluprf Ps Ind				x	Pluprf Ps Sbj				x
	Fut Prf Ps Ind				x	--				

II. PERSONAL ENDINGS

Each regular finite verb encountered in reading will contain an ending telling *who is acting* (in the active voice), or *who is being acted upon* (passive). These personal endings remain quite regular across all tenses but for the perfect active. The endings are:

	Active		Passive	
	Singular	*Plural*	*Singular*	*Plural*
1st	-ō / -m	-mus	-ōr / -r	-mur
2nd	-s	-tis	-ris	-minī
3rd	-t	-nt	-tur	-ntur

In the perfect active, the personal endings become: *-ī, -istī, -it; -imus, -istis, -ērunt.*

III. Tenses and Paradigms: Indicative

A. Present Active Indicative

The personal endings are attached to the present stem of the verb. Between the ending and the stem, a transitional vowel is usually inserted (exceptions being the 1st person sing of the I and III conjugation, where -ō attaches directly to the stem). These transitional vowels are quite consistent within each conjugation, with -a- characterising the I conjugation, -e- the II, and -i- generally used in both the III and the IV conjugations (though the third person plural of the III conjugation takes -u- in the present tenses).

I love / am loving

Conj	I	II	III	IV
infin	-āre	-ēre	-ere	-īre
Singular				
1st	-ō	-ō	-ō	-i-ō
2d	-ā-s	-ē-s	-i-s	-ī-s
3d	-a-t	-e-t	-i-t	-i-t
Plural				
1st	-ā-mus	-ē-mus	-i-mus	-ī-mus
2d	-ā-tis	-ē-tis	-i-tis	-ī-tis
3d	-a-nt	-e-nt	-u-nt	-iu-nt

Thus:

Conj	I	II	III	IV
infin	amāre to love	docēre to teach	mittere to send	audīre to hear
Singular				
1st	amō	doceō	mittō	audiō
2d	amās	docēs	mittis	audīs
3d	amat	docet	mittit	audit
Plural				
1st	amāmus	docēmus	mittimus	audīmus
2d	amātis	docētis	mittitis	audītis
3d	amant	docent	mittunt	audiunt

B. Present Passive Indicative

				I am loved / being loved
Conj	I	II	III	IV
infin	-ārī	-ērī	-ī	-īrī
			Singular		
1st	-r*	-e-or	-or	-i-or
2d	-ā-ris	-ē-ris	-e-ris	-ī-ris
3d	-ā-tur	-ē-tur	-i-tur	-ī-tur
			Plural		
1st	-ā-mur	-ē-mur	-i-mur	-ī-mur
2d	-ā-minī	-ē-minī	-i-minī	-ī-minī
3d	-a-ntur	-e-ntur	-u-ntur	-iu-ntur

*-r replaces -m, but is added to -o.

Thus:

Conj	I	II	III	IV
infin	amārī	docērī	mittī	audīrī
		Singular		
1st	amor	doceor	mittor	audior
2d	amāris	docēris	mitteris	audīris
3d	amātur	docētur	mittitur	audītur
		Plural		
1st	amāmur	docēmur	mittimur	audīmur
2d	amāminī	docēminī	mittiminī	audīminī
3d	amantur	docentur	mittuntur	audiuntur

C. Imperfect Active Indicative

The imperfect active *and* passive endings attach to the present stem with these transitional vowels for each conjugation:

I	II	III	IV
-ā-	-ē-	-ē-	-iē-

The active endings are:

I used to love / was loving

	Singular	Plural
1st	-bam	-bāmus
2d	-bās	-bātis
3d	-bat	-bant

Thus:

Conj	I	II	III	IV
	Singular			
1st	amābam	docēbam	mittēbam	audiēbam
2d	amābās	docēbās	mittēbās	audiēbās
3d	amābat	docēbat	mittēbat	audiēbat
	Plural			
1st	amābāmus	docēbāmus	mittēbāmus	audiēbāmus
2d	amābātis	docēbātis	mittēbātis	audiēbātis
3d	amābant	docēbant	mittēbant	audiēbant

D. Imperfect Passive Indicative

I used to be loved / was being loved

	Singular	Plural
1st	-bar	-bāmur
2d	-bāris	-bāminī
3d	-bātur	-bantur

Thus:

Conj	I	II	III	IV
	Singular			
1st	amābar	docēbar	mittēbar	audiēbar
2d	amābāris	docēbāris	mittēbāris	audiēbāris
3d	amābātur	docēbātur	mittēbātur	audiēbātur
	Plural			
1st	amābāmur	docēbāmur	mittēbāmur	audiēbāmur
2d	amābāminī	docēbāminī	mittēbāminī	audiēbāminī
3d	amābantur	docēbantur	mittēbantur	audiēbantur

E. Future Active Indicative

The I and II conjugations behave as expected: they take the usual transitional vowels between the present stem and endings:

			I shall love	
Transitional Vowels			*Future Act Ind Endings*	
I	II		*Singular*	*Plural*
-ā-	-ē-	*1st*	-bō	-bimus
		2d	-bis	-bitis
		3d	-bit	-bunt

Thus

Conj	I		II	
	Singular	*Plural*	*Singular*	*Plural*
1st	amābō	amābimus	docēbō	docēmus
2d	amābis	amābitis	docēbis	docēbitis
3d	amābit	amābunt	docēbit	docēbunt

The III and IV conjugations take different endings from the I and II, and the III conjugation takes no transitional vowel :

			Future Act Ind Endings	
Transitional Vowels				
III	IV		*Singular*	*Plural*
none	-i-	*1st*	-am	-ēmus
		2d	-ēs	-ētis
		3d	-et	-ent

Thus

Conj	III		IV	
	Singular	*Plural*	*Singular*	*Plural*
1st	mittam	mittēmus	audiam	audiēmus
2d	mittēs	mittētis	audiēs	audiētis
3d	mittet	mittent	audiet	audient

F. Future Passive Indicative

The passive, like the active, takes two different sets of endings, using the same transitional vowels seen above.

Transitional Vowels			I shall be loved Future Pass Ind Endings		
	I	II		Singular	Plural
	-ā-	-ē-	1st	-bor	-bimur
			2d	-beris	-biminī
			3d	-bitur	-buntur

Thus

Conj	I		II	
	Singular	Plural	Singular	Plural
1st	amābor	amābimur	docēbor	docēbimur
2d	amāberis	amābiminī	docēberis	docēbiminī
3d	amābitur	amābuntur	docēbitur	docēbuntur

The III and IV conjugations take different endings from the I and II, and the III conjugation takes no transitional vowel :

Transitional Vowels			Future Pass Ind Endings		
	IIII	IV		Singular	Plural
	none	-i-	1st	-ar	-ēmur
			2d	-ēris	-ēminī
			3d	-ētur	-entur

Thus:

Conj	III		IV	
	Singular	Plural	Singular	Plural
1st	mittar	mittēmur	audiar	audiēmur
2d	mittēris	mittēminī	audiēris	audiēminī
3d	mittētur	mittentur	audiētur	audientur

G. Perfect Active Indicative

Endings attach to the perfect stem, the third principle part of the verb. In the I and IV conjugation, the perfect stems show the usual transitional vowels plus -*v*-. The II conjugation stem will often, though not always, end in -*u*-. The III conjugation stem is irregular, though many of these will end in -*s*- or some letter with an "s" sound, such as -*x*-.

General stem endings for the Perf

I	II	III	IV
-āv-	[-u-]	irreg [s/x]	-īv-

I loved

Perfect Act Ind Endings

	Singular	Plural
1st	-ī	-imus
2d	-istī	-istis
3d	-it	-ērunt

Thus

Conj	I	II	III	IV
	Singular			
1st	amāvī	docuī	mīsī	audīvī
2d	amāvistī	docuistī	mīsistī	audīvistī
3d	amāvit	docuit	mīsit	audīvit
	Plural			
1st	amāvimus	docuimus	mīsimus	audīvimus
2d	amāvistis	docuistis	mīsistis	audīvistis
3d	amāvērunt	docuērunt	mīsērunt	audīvērunt

H. Perfect Passive Indicative

The perfect passive is a two word combination. The first word is the fourth principle part, the perfect passive participle. This is followed by the present tense of *sum*.

I was loved

	Singular	Plural
1st	ppp sum	ppp sumus
2d	ppp es	ppp estis
3d	ppp est	ppp sunt

Thus:

Conj	I	II	III	IV
	Singular			
1st	amātus sum	doctus sum	missus sum	audītus sum
2d	amātus es	doctus es	missus es	audītus es
3d	amātus est	doctus est	missus est	audītus est
	Plural			
1st	amātī sumus	doctī sumus	missī sumus	audītī sumus
2d	amātī estis	doctī estis	missī estis	audītī estis
3d	amātī sunt	doctī sunt	missī sunt	audītī sunt

I. Pluperfect Active Indicative

The pluperfect active endings are identical to the imperfect of *sum*. These are attached to the perfect stem, which will include the same transitional configurations as were seen in the perfect tense, above:

I had loved

Gnl stem endings for the Plperf

I	II	III	IV
-āv-	[-u-]	irreg [s/x]	-īv-

Pluperfect Act Ind Endings

	Singular	*Plural*
1st	-eram	-erāmus
2d	-erās	-erātis
3d	-erat	-erant

Thus:

Conj	I	II	III	IV
	Singular			
1st	amāveram	docueram	mīseram	audīveram
2d	amāverās	docuerās	mīserās	audīverās
3d	amāverat	docuerat	mīserat	audīverat
	Plural			
1st	amāverāmus	docuerāmus	mīserāmus	audīverāmus
2d	amāverātis	docuerātis	mīserātis	audīverātis
3d	amāverant	docuerant	mīserant	audīverant

J. Pluperfect Passive Indicative

The pluperfect passive, like the perfect passive, consists of two words, the first being the perfect passive participle of the verb. The second word is the imperfect of *sum*. Thus:

I had been loved

Conj	I	II	III	IV
			Singular		
1st	amātus eram	doctus eram	missus eram	audītus eram
2d	amātus erās	doctus erās	missus erās	audītus erās
3d	amātus erat	doctus erat	missus erat	audītus erat
			Plural		
1st	amātī erāmus	doctī erāmus	missī erāmus	audītī erāmus
2d	amātī erātis	doctī erātis	missī erātis	audītī erātis
3d	amātī erant	doctī erant	missī erant	audītī erant

K. Future Perfect Indicative

Active: I shall have loved; Passive: I shall have been loved

The future perfect tense is quite rare and can be summarised here quickly. The active endings consist of the future of *sum* attached to the perfect stem. The single exception here is the third person plural where *-erunt* becomes *-erint*. The passive is based on the same pattern seen in the perfect and pluperfect passive: the perfect passive participle is followed by a second word, in this case the future of *sum*.

IV. Tenses and Paradigms: Subjunctive

The general use of the subjunctive suggests a possibility that may or may not become a reality. Its translation into English is highly contextual.

The subjunctive occurs in the present, the imperfect, the perfect and the pluperfect. Of these, the imperfect and the pluperfect are somewhat more common.

A. Present Active Subjunctive

The endings below are affixed to the present stem, but with one minor adjustment. There are two sets of endings. The first set is used only for the I conjugation, and the transitional vowel -a- disappears, replaced by the -e- of the ending. The second set of endings is used on all other conjugations, as usual.

	Conjugation I		Conjugation II, III, IV	
	Singular	**Plural**	**Singular**	**Plural**
1st	-em	-ēmus	-am	-āmus
2d	-ēs	-ētis	-ās	-ātis
3d	-et	-ent	-at	-ant

Thus:

Conj	I	II	III	IV
	Singular			
1st	amem	doceam	mittam	audiam
2d	amēs	doceās	mittās	audiās
3d	amet	doceat	mittat	audiat
	Plural			
1st	amēmus	doceāmus	mittāmus	audiāmus
2d	amētis	doceātis	mittātis	audiātis
3d	ament	doceant	mittant	audiant

B. Present Passive Subjunctive

These endings are affixed to the present stem. As in the active, the usual -a- ending of the I Conjugation is, replaced by the -e-.

	Conjugation I		Conjugation II, III, IV	
	Singular	**Plural**	**Singular**	**Plural**
1st	-er	-ēmur	-ar	-āmur
2d	-ēris	-ēminī	-āris	-āminī
3d	-ētur	-entur	-ātur	-antur

Conj	I	II	III	IV
	Singular			
1st	amer	docear	mittar	audiar
2d	amēris	doceāris	mittāris	audiāris
3d	amētur	doceātur	mittātur	audiātur
	Plural			
1st	amēmur	doceāmur	mittāmur	audiāmur
2d	amēminī	doceāminī	mittāminī	audiāminī
3d	amentur	doceantur	mittantur	audiantur

C. Imperfect Active Subjunctive

The imperfect active subjunctive is formed quite regularly and simply. The standard personal endings for the active voice are added directly to the present infinitive (the second principle part of the verb), employed as a stem.

Conj	I	II	III	IV
	Singular			
1st	-āre-m	-ēre-m	-ere-m	-īre-m
2d	-ārē-s	-ērē-s	-erē-s	-īrē-s
3d	-āre-t	-ēre-t	-ere-t	-īre-t
	Plural			
1st	-ārē-mus	-ērē-mus	-erē-mus	-īrē-mus
2d	-ārē-tis	-ērē-tis	-erē-tis	-īrē-tis
3d	-āre-nt	-ēre-nt	-ere-nt	-īre-nt

Thus:

Conj	I	II	III	IV
	Singular			
1st	amārem	docērem	mitterem	audīrem
2d	amārēs	docērēs	mitterēs	audīrēs
3d	amāret	docēret	mitteret	audīret
	Plural			
1st	amārēmus	docērēmus	mitterēmus	audīrēmus
2d	amārētis	docērētis	mitterētis	audīrētis
3d	amārent	docērent	mitterent	audīrent

D. Imperfect Passive Subjunctive

The imperfect passive subjunctive is, like the active voice, quite regular. The standard personal endings for the passive voice are simply added directly onto the second principle part, the present active infinitive.

Conj	I	II	III	IV
	Singular			
1st	-āre-r	-ēre-r	-ere-r	-īre-r
2d	-ārē-is	-ērē-ris	-ere-ris	-īrē-ris
3d	-ārē-tur	-ērē-tur	-ere-tur	-īrē-tur
	Plural			
1st	-ārē-mur	-ērē-mur	-ere-mur	-īrē-mur
2d	-ārē-minī	-ērē-minī	-ere-minī	-īrē-minī
3d	-āre-ntur	-ēre-ntur	-ere-ntur	-īre-ntur

Thus:

Conj	I	II	III	IV
	Singular			
1st	amārer	docērer	mitterer	audīrer
2d	amārēs	docērēris	mitterēris	audīrēris
3d	amārētur	docērētur	mitterētur	audīrētur
	Plural			
1st	amārēmur	docērēmur	mitterēmur	audīrēmur
2d	amārēminī	docērēminī	mitterēminī	audīrēminī
3d	amārentur	docērentur	mitterentur	audīrentur

D. Perfect Active Subjunctive

These endings are attached to the perfect stem:

	Singular	Plural
1st	-erim	-erīmus
2d	-erīs	-erītis
3d	-erit	-erint

Thus:

Conj	I	II	III	IV
	Singular			
1st	amāverim	docuerim	mīserim	audīverim
2d	amāverīs	docuerīs	mīserīs	audīverīs
3d	amāverit	docuerit	mīserit	audīverit
	Plural			
1st	amāverīmus	docuerīmus	mīserīmus	audīverīmus
2d	amāverītis	docuerītis	mīserītis	audīverītis
3d	amāverint	docuerint	mīserint	audīverint

E. Perfect Passive Subjunctive

The perfect passive participle is followed with the present subjunctive of *sum*, appearing as a separate word. Thus:

Conj	I	II	III	IV
	Singular			
1st	amātus sim	doctus sim	missus sim	audītus sim
2d	amātus sīs	doctus sīs	missus sīs	audītus sīs
3d	amātus sit	doctus sit	missus sit	audītus sit
	Plural			
1st	amātī sīmus	doctī sīmus	missī sīmus	audītī sīmus
2d	amātī sītis	doctī sītis	missī sītis	audītī sītis
3d	amātī sint	doctī sint	missī sint	audītī sint

E. Pluperfect Active Subjunctive

The formation of the pluperfect active subjunctive mirrors the formation of the imperfect active subjunctive with one change. The *present* infinitive served as the stem of the imperfect subjunctive, while the *perfect* infinitive serves as the stem here. (The perfect active infinitive is derived by adding *-isse* to the perfect stem.) The standard personal endings are simply attached to the perfect active infinitive, used as the stem.

Conj	I	II	III	IV
	Singular			
1st	-āvisse-m	-uisse-m	-isse-m	-īvisse-m
2d	-āvissē-s	-uissē-s	-issē-s	-īvissē-s
3d	-āvisse-t	-uisse-t	-isse-t	-īvisse-t
	Plural			
1st	-āvissē-mus	-uissē-mus	-issē-mus	-īvissē-mus
2d	-āvissē-tis	-uissē-tis	-issē-tis	-īvissē-tis
3d	-āvisse-nt	-uisse-nt	-isse-nt	-īvisse-nt

Thus:

Conj	I	II	III	IV
	Singular			
1st	amāvissem	docuissem	mīsissem	audīvissem
2d	amāvissēs	docuissēs	mīsissēs	audīvissēs
3d	amāvisset	docuisset	mīsisset	audīvisset
	Plural			
1st	amāvissēmus	docuissēmus	mīsissēmus	audīvissēmus
2d	amāvissētis	docuissētis	mīsissētis	audīvissētis
3d	amāvissent	docuissent	mīsissent	audīvissent

F. Pluperfect Passive Subjunctive

The pluperfect passive subjunctive takes the perfect passive participle and follows this with the imperfect subjunctive of *sum*, appearing as a separate word.

	Singular		Plural	
1st	ppp essem		ppp essēmus	
2d	ppp essēs		ppp essētis	
3d	ppp esset		ppp essent	

Thus:

Conj	I	II	III	IV
	Singular			
1st	amātus essem	doctus essem	missus essem	audītus essem
2d	amātus essēs	doctus essēs	missus essēs	audītus essēs
3d	amātus esset	doctus esset	missus esset	audītus esset
	Plural			
1st	amātī essēmus	doctī essēmus	missī essēmus	audītī essēmus
2d	amātī essētis	doctī essētis	missī essētis	audītī essētis
3d	amātī essent	doctī essent	missī essent	audītī essent

187

CHAPTER 6

MEDIAEVAL TERMS

In his dissertation, Diederich notes the appeal of Mediaeval Latin, especially for beginning students. Sentence structure, he observes, is often simpler, but at the same time the Mediaeval literature "was written in authentic Latin by men who spoke and thought in Latin, with the ring of genuine communication in it." He highlights the student's need for "easy and interesting material . . . that is worth reading" and suggests that "an almost inexhaustible supply of such material" is to be found in the Latin of the Middle Ages.

Too often, the vocabulary of the Mediaeval literature is assumed to be too remote and too different from Classical Latin to be of genuine use. While that may be true of some technical fields such as law, it is not so in most ordinary texts, as Diederich shows in his first chapter. By learning little more than 80 new words—many of them easily recognized—students will find another 1,000 years of Latin literature at their command, and their vocabulary will be as efficient in the literature of the Middle Ages as it is in the Classical era.

The following 100 words occur with an increased frequency within Mediaeval texts. Some are obviously derived from the new religion of Christianity and its practices (abbās, e.g.). Others have undergone subtle changes reflecting different cultural situations (cf. palātium), while yet others inexplicably appear as statistically significant in the Mediaeval era but less significant in the Classical period (vīginti, e.g.). Regardless of the reason, these are 100 of the most statistically important terms that appear within Mediaeval Latin at a rate not found in the Classical world.

The words are presented first with their definitions, and second in an index, giving the term, its part of speech, grammatical classification, and frequency based on how often one would see the term within a 1,000 words of typical Mediaeval Latin. Within the index, indented terms are less frequent, but are closely related to the term immediately above.

I. Terms and Definitions

abbās, -ātis	abbot, head of an ecclesiastical community; *early:* any hermit or esteemed monk; father, spiritual father
abbātia, -ae	abbey, monastery
abbātissa, -ae	abbess, head of a nunnery
aditus, -ūs	an opening, access, entrance; audience, interview, access
admīror, -ari, -ātus sum	to wonder at, admire, be astonished at. This is a state of mind inspired by the sublime; cf. *mirari* which is to be surprised at something novel or unusual
aedificō, -āre, -āvi, -ātus	to build, create; improve; edify
aestimō, -āre, -āvi, -ātus	to value, assess, appraise; estimate moral worth of a thing; intrinsic value of an object for the sake of fines
alleluia	cry of praise to God
altāria, -āris	that placed on the altar for sacrifice; the victim
amārus, -a, -um	bitter, brackish, harsh, shrill; calamitous, sad
ambulo, -āre, -āvī, -ātus	to walk, take a walk; travel, march; strut
angelus, -ī	angel, messenger
antequam	before, sooner than; until
ānulus, -ī	signet ring; circlet; link of mail; fetters, irons; the anus
argentum, -ī	silver; money
arripio, -ere, -cēpī, -ceptus	to take hold of; arrest; summon before a tribunal
benedīcō, -ere, dīxī, dictus	to bless; speak well of
bestia, -ae	beast, animal
cāritas, -ātis	charity; love affection, esteem

caro, carnis	flesh; seat of the passions (opp to spirit); pulp of trees, fruits
cella, -ae	a cell, monastic dwelling; storeroom; sanctuary; pen
Christus, -ī	Christ
Christiānē	in a Christian way
Christiānus, -a, -um	Christian
Christiānitas, -ātis	Christianity
claustrum, -ī	bolt, gate; monastery, cloister (oft. Pl)
clēricus, -ī	clergyman, priest, cleric, clerk; student, scholar, scribe
comedo, -ōnis	glutton
consīderō, -āre, -āvī, -ātus	to examine, inspect; consider closely; investigate
cōram (+Ab)	in the presence of, before; personally; as adv., face-to-face, before one's eyes; publicly, openly
crux, crucis	cross; crucifixion
crucifīgō, -fīgere, -fīxī, -fīxus	to crucify
crucifīxus, -fixi	crucifix, *smtms* -um, -ixi, Nt
custōdio, -īre, -iī (-īvī), -itus	to watch, protect, defend
daemon, -onis	demon, devil
daemonicola, -ae	heathen, worshipper of devils
daemoniocus, -a, -um	demonic; *subst:* one possessed by an evil spirit
diabolus, -ī	devil; the Devil, Satan
discipulus, -ī	student; follower, disciple
doctrīna, -ae	teaching, instruction; learning, erudition
doctrīnālis, -āle	doctrinal, theoretical
ecclēsia, -ae	church; assembly of Christians
ēligō, -ere, -lēg -ī, -lctus	to pick out, pluck out; to choose
emittō, -ere, -mīsī, -missus	to let go; expel; discharge; cast

epīscopus, -ī	bishop; an overseer
expendō, -ere, -pendī, -pēnsus	to weigh out; pay
expōnō, -ere, -posuī, -positus	to set out, set forth, explain, expose; abandon; disembark
festinō, -āre, -āvī, -ātus	to hurry, hasten;
fūr, fūris	thief
hodiē	today
indūcō, -ere, -dūxī, -dctus	lead in, bring in; bring before a court; induce; introduce
insula, -ae	island; block of apartments
interrogō, -āre, -āvī, -ātus	to interrogate, question; indict; *smtms:* sue
invitō, -āre, -āvī, -ātus	to invite, treat, entertain; summon, challenge
item	likewise, moreover
iuxtā (juxtā)	near; after, according to; per; in proportion to
laetitia, -ae	joy; unrestrained delight, gladness
lignum, -ī	wood; something made of wood, e.g., writing tablet, spear shaft; a plank; shell of a nut, stone of a fruit
ligō, -āre, -āvī, -ātus	bind, tie, fasten; unite, bring together
medicus, -a, -um	healing, curative;
meditor, -ārī, -ātus sum	contemplate, ponder; meditate, reflect on; devise, plan
misericordia, -ae	mercy, pity, compassion, tender-heartedness
monachus, -ī	monk
monastērium, -iī	monastery
nāvigō, -āre, -āvī, -ātus	to sail
nutriō, -īre, -īvī, -ītus	nourish, suckle, feed; foster, rear, bring up
oleum, -ī	oil

ostium, -ī	doorway; entrance (oft., to underworld); mouth of a river
palātium, -ī	king's court; the royal palace
pānis, pānis	bread, loaf
persōna -ae	mask; character, personality
philosophus -a -um	philosophical
philosophus -i	philosopher
pōtus, -ūs	a drink, draught; drinking (intoxicating drink)
praedicō, -ere, -dīxī, -dictus	warn, predict, foretell; recommend, prescribe
praedīcō, -āre, -āvī, -ātus	proclaim, declare, announce; praise; preach
praesentia, -ae	presence; present time
praeparō, -āre, -āvī, -ātus	to prepare
presbyter, -terī	elder in Christian Church; priest
pretiōsus, -a, -um	precious, of great value, valuable
prūdens, -entis	skilled, experienced; post Aug., valiant, brave
quattuor; quartus, -a, -um	four
redimo, -dimere, -dēmi, -demptus	redeem, buy back, recover, replace by purchase; fulfill a promise
religiōsus -a -um	pious, devout, religious, scrupulous; superstitious; taboo, sacred; reverent
remaneō, -ere, -ansi, -ansus	to stay behind; be left; endure
rēpleo, -ēre, -ēvī, -ētus	to fill again
sapiens, -entis	wise; a member of the city council
scientia -ae	knowledge, science; skill
status status	mode; position, situation, condition; rank
superveniō, -īre, vēnī, ventus	to come over or upon; to fall upon; to come up
suscipio, -cipere, -cēpi, -ceptus	to undertake; support; accept

thēsaurus, -ī	treasure; anything stored up
transmittō, -ere, -mīsī, -missus	to carry over, carry through, convey across; to send off, dispatch, pass along from one to another
valdē	intensely; vigorously; loudly
vas, vasis	vessel; vase; kit; utensil
venter, -tris	stomach; womb
vēritas, veritātis	truth, fact; the true or real nature; sincerity; truthfulness
vesper, -eris (also as -eri)	evening; the evening office of prayer
vestīmentum, -ī	garment, vestment
vīginti; vicēsimus -a -um,	twenty

II. INDEX OF MEDIAEVAL TERMS

abbās, -ātis	n	3m	0.84
abbātia, -ae	n	1f	
abbātissa, -ae	n	1f	
aditus, -ūs	n	4m	0.27
admīror, -ari, -ātus sum	v	1d	0.34
aedificō, -āre, -āvi, -ātus	v	1	0.32
aestimō, -āre, -āvi, -ātus	v	1.00	0.26
alleluia	intrj	ind	0.72
altāria, -āris	n	3n	0.28
amārus, -a, -um	adj	212	0.26
ambulo, -āre, -āvī, -ātus	v	1	0.26
angelus, -ī	n	2m	0.53
antequam	cnj	ind	0.27
ānulus, -ī	n	2m	0.34
argentum, -ī	n	2n	0.44
arripio, -ere, -cēpī, -ceptus	v	3	0.30
benedīcō, -ere, dīxī, dictus	v	3	0.49

bestia, -ae	n	1f	0.26
cāritas, -ātis	n	3f	0.39
caro, carnis	n	3f	0.32
cella, -ae	n	1f	0.26
Christus, -ī	n	2m	1.02
Christiānē	adv	ind	
Christiānus, -a, -um	adj	212	
Christiānitas, -ātis	n	3f	
claustrum, -ī	n	2n	0.30
clēricus, -ī	n	2m	0.35
comedo, -ōnis	n	3m	0.67
consīderō, -āre, -āvī, -ātus	v	1	0.30
cōram (+Ab)	prep	ind	0.61
crux, crucis	n	3f	0.27
crucifīgō, -fīgere, -fīxī, -fīxus	v	3	
crucifīxus, -fixi	n	2m	
custōdio, -īre, -iī (-īvī), -itus	v	4	0.32
daemon, -onis	n	3m	0.30
daemonicola, -ae	n	1f	
daemoniocus, -a, -um	adj	212	
diabolus, -ī	n	2m	0.35
discipulus, -ī	n	2m	0.30
doctrīna, -ae	n	1f	0.31
doctrīnālis, -āle	adj	3-2	
ecclēsia, -ae	n	1f	0.90
ēligō, -ere, -lēg -ī, -lctus	v	3	0.75
emittō, -ere, -mīsī, -missus	v	3	0.30
epīscopus, -ī	n	2m	0.57
expendō, -ere, -pendī, -pēnsus	v	3	0.32
expōnō, -ere, -posuī, -positus	v	3	0.31
festinō, -āre, -āvī, -ātus	v	1	0.36
fūr, fūris	n	3mf	0.43
hodiē	adv	ind	0.41

indūcō, -ere, -dūxī, -dctus	v	3	0.32
insula, -ae	n	1f	0.27
interrogō, -āre, -āvī, -ātus	v	1	0.53
invitō, -āre, -āvī, -ātus	v	1	0.31
item	adv	ind	0.70
iuxtā (juxtā)	adv	ind	0.44
laetitia, -ae	n	1f	0.30
lignum, -ī	n	2m	0.43
ligō, -āre, -āvī, -ātus	v	1	0.28
medicus, -a, -um	adj	212	0.26
meditor, -ārī, -ātus sum	v	1d	0.28
misericordia, -ae	n	1f	0.26
monachus, -ī	n	m	0.26
monastērium, -iī	n	2n	0.98
nāvigō, -āre, -āvī, -ātus	v	1	0.67
nutriō, -īre, -īvī, -ītus	v	4	0.45
oleum, -ī	n	2m	0.26
ostium, -ī	n	2n	0.35
palatium, -ī	n	2n	0.36
pānis, pānis	n	3m	0.44
persōna -ae	n	1f	0.35
philosophus -a -um	adj	212	0.52
philosophus -i	n	2m	
pōtus, -ūs	n	4m	0.28
praedicō, -ere, -dīxī, -dictus	v	3	0.26
praedīcō, -āre, -āvī, -ātus	v	1	0.48
praesentia, -ae	n	1f	0.36
praeparō, -āre, -āvī, -ātus	v	1	0.28
presbyter, -terī	n	2m	0.46
pretiōsus, -a, -um	adj	ind	0.26
prūdens, -entis	adj	3-1	0.31
quattuor; quartus, -a, -um	adj	irr	0.46
redimo, -dimere, -dēmi, -demptus	v	3	0.26

religiōsus -a -um	adj	212	0.28
remaneō, -ere, -ansi, -ansus	v	2	0.40
rēpleo, -ēre, -ēvī, -ētus	v	3	0.26
sapiens, -entis	adj	3-1	0.53
scientia -ae	n	1f	0.59
status status	n	4m	0.30
superveniō, -īre, vēnī, ventus	v	4	0.48
suscipio, -cipere, -cēpi, -ceptus	v	3	0.32
thēsaurus, -ī	n	2m	0.52
transmittō, -ere, mīsī, missus	v	3	0.26
valdē	adv	ind	0.75
vas, vasis	n	3n	0.31
venter, -tris	n	m	0.39
vēritas, veritātis	n	3f	0.30
vesper, -eris	n	3m	0.30
vestīmentum, -ī	n	2n	0.26
vīginti; vicēsimus -a -um,	adj	irr	0.35

Sophron

with

Made in the USA
Middletown, DE
04 April 2019